# BEGINNER'S GUIDE

# PAINTING IN
# *Pastels*

## JENNY RODWELL

STUDIO
VISTA

## ACKNOWLEDGEMENTS

The author and publishers would like to thank the following artists who have allowed
us to use their work in this book: John Crawford Fraser, p. 10; Charmian Edgerton,
pp. 7, 11, 12, 76–7; Graham Painter, pp. 6–7, 10, 13, 70–1; Adrian Paschal Smith,
p. 9; Frances Treanor, pp. 8–9, 42, 43. Special thanks to Unison for their generous help
with materials; to Charmian Edgerton and Ian Sidaway for their step-by-step
demonstrations and artwork; and to Fred Munden for taking the photographs.

Studio Vista
an imprint of
Cassell
Villiers House
41/47 Strand
London WC2N 5JE

First published 1993

British Library Cataloguing-in-Publication Data
A catalogue record for this book is available from the British Library.

ISBN 0-289-80073-0

Series editors: Jenny Rodwell and Patricia Monahan
The moral rights of the author have been asserted

Series designer Edward Pitcher

Distributed in the United States by
Sterling Publishing Co. Inc.
387 Park Avenue South, New York, NY 10016-8810

Typeset by Litho Link Ltd., Welshpool, Powys

Printed in Great Britain by
Bath Colourbooks, Glasgow

# CONTENTS

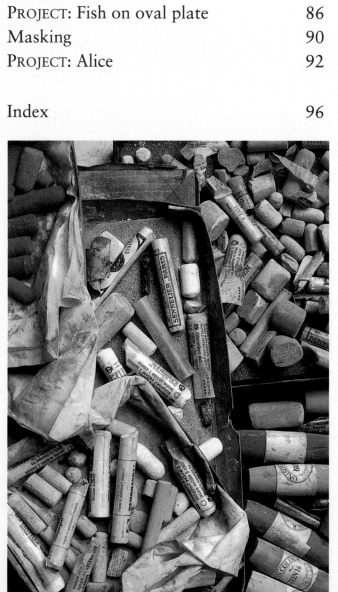

# Pastel painting

PASTELS ARE USED frequently by professionals; yet they are also ideal for the beginner. 'Once you start using pastels you become addicted,' says professional pastel painter Charmian Edgerton. 'It is a dry medium. You do not have to mix it to make it work, and there is a tremendous range of ready-to-use colours and tones, offering brilliant colours and a great deal of subtlety at the same time.'

While the professional makes use of the extensive range of pastels, the beginner is able to take advantage of the fact that the colour-mixing has already been done by the manufacturer. The equivalent of the oil-painter's 'palette' is a large assortment of manufactured colour combinations – pale pink and dark red, for example, as well as the pure red from which the pale and dark versions would otherwise have had to be mixed.

It is not until you use pastels that you realize they are more than just sticks to draw with – they are very much a 'painting' medium. The sticks are used to build up areas of tone and colour rather than merely to draw lines. As with oil and acrylic paints, you can lay down an area of colour, then add more opaque colours in certain places, to create an increasingly subtle image. This is why pastel works are referred to as paintings, not drawings.

Unlike paints, pastel is a dry medium, and you can apply each colour instantly without having to wait for the rest of the painting to dry out. This artist works quickly on a flower painting, laying successive colours in rapid, spontaneous strokes.

# THE SCOPE

Pastels as we know them have been in use since the early eighteenth century. In comparison with paints, the origins of which can be traced back to prehistoric times, this makes pastels a very new medium indeed.

In the days before pastels, harder chalks and crayons bound with oil or wax were sometimes used – commonly on a tinted ground. But these early materials were for drawing only, and were available in a very limited range of colours, usually black, white and earth red. This is far removed from the enormous range of products currently on offer.

Today it is possible to go to an art shop and choose from over 500 colours. You can buy hard pastels, soft pastels, pastel pencils, delicately slim pastels, and pastels as thick as your wrist. In addition to this, a wide variety of papers and boards specially made for use with pastels in a range of colours and textures for all requirements is also available.

There is no absolutely correct way to use pastels: the medium is versatile and lends itself to many different techniques and approaches. Their chunkiness makes pastels ideal for working on a large scale and for loose renderings of almost any subject, yet they can also be used in a completely different and much finer way. For instance, many pastel paintings are so detailed that they are indistinguishable from coloured photographs.

**Drawing or painting**

It is because pastels come in stick form that people tend to think of them as a drawing medium. They look rather like the coloured chalks used at school, so it is assumed that they are for making lines rather than for creating areas of solid colour. And, of course, some artists do use pastels mainly for drawing, taking advantage of the wide range of colours as well as of the many different types of line that can be made with the various pastels available.

But by far the majority of artists who work in pastels use them as a painting medium, building up

the rich, crumbling pigments to create the same solid, vibrant images that we see in oils, acrylics, gouaches and other paintings. But instead of applying colour in liquid form, as with these paints, pastel artists use the dry sticks for laying areas of bold colour; for building up thick layers of pigment; and for putting one layer of colour over another – all of which are techniques traditionally associated with painting rather than drawing. For this reason, pastel artists almost always refer to their works as 'paintings', not 'drawings'.

◁ **Wild Flowers** *Soft pastels are applied in free, loose strokes to create the windswept flowers and corn in this landscape by artist Graham Painter. The composition is informal and unstructured – a good example of soft pastels at their spontaneous best.*

△ **Roses in a Stone Jar** *Charmian Edgerton works by building up layer upon layer of pastel pigment to create the subtle colours of her subjects. Her work is painstaking and time-consuming; this particular painting took about five weeks to complete.*

# VERSATILE PASTEL

For the beginner, the great advantage of pastels is that they can be extremely simple to use. With just a few colours and a sheet of paper, you can tackle any subject and produce a lively painting full of texture and colour. Another bonus is that pastels are applied dry; you do not have to mix or dilute the pigments with water, oil or any other liquid.

However, pastel also works on a more sophisticated level. As your skills improve, the same pastels will offer infinite scope and the opportunity to experiment with an extended palette and more ambitious techniques.

### Line and colour

Probably one of the most accomplished pastel artists who ever lived was the Frenchman Edgar Degas (1834–1917). For him the medium had no limits. Not only could he describe the form, tone and colour of his subject – every bit as well as he could with oil paints – but pastels also allowed him to introduce line and contour into his painting. As a result, superb draughtsmanship enhances the painterly content of his figures as he traces the flowing forms and sinewy outlines of his human subjects.

Degas also taught us how to build up subtle areas of colour with pastel. Human skin is infinitely varied in its tone and colour. Subtle pinks, yellows, blues, mauves and greens are present in all flesh tones. With paints, we can but mix and apply these, blob by blob, in an overall approximation of what we see before us. With pastels, it is possible to overlay these colours, one on top of another, thus capturing not only the subtle hues but also the characteristic glow and transparency of human flesh tones.

The two paintings here are very diverse – two examples of how pastels can express totally different aspects of a subject. One is done purely in line, not realistically but using the colours symbolically to give an exaggerated view of colour and form. The second is more naturalistic, the

building up of observed colour and tone to create a real and convincing rendition of the floral still-life subject.

No one way of working is better or more appropriate than another. Whether you use them as a drawing medium or for building up areas of colour, pastels are the means to an end, and the end can be whatever you, the artist, want it to be.

◁ **Vase of Irises** *For Frances Treanor, shape and colour are the important aspects of any subject. Her work is intricately designed, and these flowers are depicted mainly in terms of shape and colour. As well as providing a range of brilliant hues, pastels allow the artist to introduce strokes of broad texture into areas of strong, vibrant colours. The decorative border is a personal touch, used to emphasize the decorative elements in the subject.*

Such a wide range of possibilities makes pastels one of the most exciting media available to the painters of today. It also accounts for the increasing popularity of pastels with beginners and experienced artists alike. And it is no coincidence that the majority of pastel painters turn to pastels after working for several years in another medium, usually oils or watercolour.

△ **Woman Resting** *Pastels can be used for drawing as well as for laying areas of colour and tone. In this portrait, Adrian Smith exploits line and colour creatively rather than literally in order to convey his impression of the subject.*

# CHOOSING A SUBJECT

It is important to like what you are painting. This could be a figure, a landscape, a favourite corner of your home or an arrangement of objects brought together for the purpose of the picture. Really, the subject does not matter provided it inspires you.

## Make it simple

As a newcomer to the medium you would be wise to avoid anything too complicated. After all, you are getting to grips with new materials; there is no need to make extra problems for yourself by picking the most difficult possible subject to start off with.

That said, any subject can be simplified. A landscape, for instance, is rarely simple in itself, because it contains so many different elements, textures and colours. Yet it can be made simple because soft, chunky pastels allow you to ignore detail and to go for the broad aspects of a scene.

A good example of this approach is the step-by-step project painting starting on page 64. Here the artist concentrates on sweeping areas of colour – the sky, hills and lavender fields – rather than on individual plants and trees. The painting is an uncomplicated arrangement of coloured, textured shapes, almost abstract in concept yet still conveying vividly the atmosphere and character of the subject.

## Small is beautiful

An alternative to simplification is to tackle a small part of the subject. Just as a photographer might use a close-up lens to zoom in on a microscopic detail of a much wider landscape, so you can choose a tiny fragment of the whole and make it into a complete composition. Graham Painter's poppy field, illustrated here, is just such a picture. He has 'zoomed in' on an autumnal landscape, choosing a colourful detail and making it into a landscape in its own right.

Still-life subjects are particularly versatile in this

respect. In this case you have absolute control, and can arrange the subject entirely to your liking. Colours, shapes and patterns can be picked up and tried, then accepted or rejected until you have the arrangement you want. This can be as simple and minimal as necessary. A single object, or even part of an object, can make a totally satisfactory subject for a painting.

The very first project in this book is a simple monochrome still life – a perfectly straightforward arrangement of fruit on a checked tablecloth. Yet the subject gave the artist plenty of opportunity to paint as he wanted – in this case, using a range of tones with no colour. As he set up the subject, each item was chosen for its tonal value and shape – for the contribution it would make to the painting.

This is an example of how you are not necessarily committed to painting 'what is there'. You can select those aspects of a landscape, still life or figure which make the subject work as a painting. And this need not be an accurate representation of everything you can see.

◁ **Figure**  *Pastel can be used with great delicacy and subtlety, as this figure painting by John Crawford-Fraser demonstrates. There is very little colour in the subject or the finished painting; bright light and strong shadow are depicted mainly in black, white and grey. The background, though lightly indicated, is particularly important because it describes the space in which the dancer moves.*

▽ **Still life**  *An unusual and creative composition gives added interest to this simple arrangement of objects. Still-life painting allows the artist absolute control over both the subject and the finished image, and the initial planning can be as important as the actual painting.*

◁ **Landscape**  *For centuries the elements of landscape have been portrayed by artists in many different ways. In this case, the painter chose a deliberately simple composition; the main emphasis of the work lies in the lively movement and texture of the wide expanse of foreground grass.*

# PLANNING THE COMPOSITION

A good composition is one that looks effortless and natural but has, nevertheless, been carefully planned. Well-composed pictures attract and hold our attention without getting in the way of our enjoyment of the painting, and without making us aware of why the composition works.

A poor or clumsy composition, on the other hand, is immediately noticeable, usually for very obvious reasons, and fails to captivate the viewer.

### Consider the background

The first rule of composition is to plan the picture as a whole, paying as much attention to the background as to the main subject. This is particularly true of figure and still-life paintings, when it is easy to get carried away with the central subject and forget about the equally important surroundings. A subject must be placed in context, and given a space and environment in which to exist.

Students doing life drawing for the first time tend to make one of two basic errors. Often, they start drawing without first planning whether or not the figure will fit on to the paper. Typically, they begin by drawing the head either too big or too low down on the support. Then – often quite subconsciously – the rest of the figure gets smaller and smaller in an effort to keep it on the paper. When they stand back to look at the finished drawing, the lower half of the body and legs look hopelessly out of proportion, squashed in by the bottom edge of the paper.

The other, equally common, mistake is to make the subject too small – a tiny, floating figure surrounded by masses of empty paper. The problem here is that our eyes and common sense tell us that the paper is flat, although the figure is drawn as a three-dimensional object. Not only is the empty background space failing to contribute to the composition; but it is actually detracting from the figure itself.

However, both these scenarios are easily avoided with a little advanced planning.

### 'Closed' compositions

A classical composition is one is which the viewer's eye is attracted and held within the painting. Generally, an artist achieves this by arranging the subject in such a way that the shapes, tones and colours invite our eye to move from place to place within the confines of the picture area. A good example of this classical, or 'closed', type of composition is the painting of the flower and chair illustrated here.

▷ **'Closed' composition** *A dominant feature here is the cascading flower basket which hangs down from the top of the painting. The eye picks up these downward shapes, which then transfer the gaze around the curved chair and back to the flowers. Thus the viewer's attention is held in a circular movement in the central part of the painting.*

In the work, the subject is completely contained within the picture area. There are no discordant shapes; nothing is half in and half out of the painting. Instead, our gaze is encouraged to move around within the picture. It is drawn from the hanging basket, down around the curved shape of the chair, and then gently upwards again back to the basket.

In a typically 'closed' composition, the corners of a rectangular or square painting are often redundant because the main activity takes place in a circular or oval shape in the central area of the support.

### The 'open' alternative
An 'open' composition contains nothing to impede the eye as it moves around and across the composition. Many painters employ this device to create a sense of space in their paintings, to convey the idea that the scene continues outside the

△ **'Open' composition**  *When there is nothing in a painting to hold or guide the attention of the viewer, it is often referred to as an 'open' composition. Such paintings are generally characterized by a sense of space and light – as is the watery scene illustrated here.*

confines of the picture. By their very nature, many landscapes fall into this category.

The waterscape illustrated here works well in this respect. It is a typically open composition, with no sharp or intrusive shapes to impede the viewer's eye as it moves across the surface of the picture.

Some 'open' compositions appear to have little or no formal structure at all. The poppy painting on pages 6 and 7 is purely concerned with colour and texture; there are no sharp contrasts or dominant shapes to interfere with the open nature of the composition.

*13*

# Materials

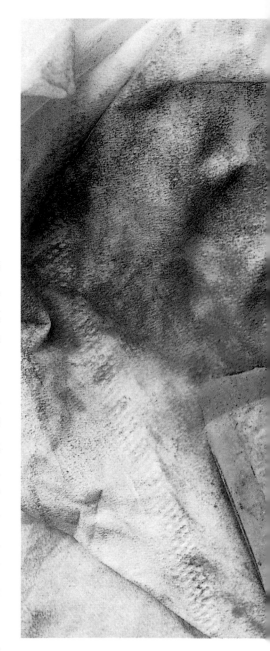

ONE OF THE great advantages of working with pastels is that you do not require an elaborate set of materials, needing no more than the sticks of pastel and something to paint on. This is in no way a limitation, because you have before you a vast range of pastels to explore.

Part of the skill of the pastel painter lies in seeking out and developing the potential of specific pastels. Manufacturers are constantly working on the particular properties that characterize their brands. One, for instance, might have a certain range of greens, or reds, which suits your individual requirements. Some brands are distinctively soft; others have a consistently velvety texture. This book gives you a glimpse of a pastel factory to help your understanding of materials and to show how creative the process of pastel-making can be.

The colour and texture of pastel papers play an important part in a finished painting, and a large variety of different coloured papers is available. However, you will probably want to add to this, so this book will introduce you to different ways of tinting and colouring paper, and of creating your own textured surfaces.

Pastel materials are a very simple matter because all you really need to start are a few colours and a sheet of card or paper on which to paint. However, as your experience and enthusiasm increase, so will your needs. Many pastel artists, for instance, have a collection of several hundred pastels – a colour and tone to suit every occasion!

# PASTELS

The way to make sense of the vast range of types of pastel now available is to divide them all into two main groups – hard and soft. But it is important to remember that within each group there are degrees of hardness and softness – the uninitiated can become quite confused when they hear an artist talking about 'hard' soft pastels.

### Hard pastels

Hard pastels contain more gum than soft ones, which makes them less powdery and malleable. They come in compressed sticks, often rectangular in shape, and include some of the Conté range, and Nu-Pastels, made by Eberhard-Faber.

### Soft pastels

Soft pastels are characteristically crumbly, and are usually chunkier than those in the hard group. They include Sennelier, Unison, LeFranc and Bourgeois, Carb-Othello, Rowney and Grumbacher.

The soft pastels come in greatly varying sizes, with some manufacturers producing more than a single size. Unison, for example, make a very chunky stick along with a smaller size; Sennelier produce a 'giant' pastel as well as their standard one. The giants, available in a limited range of colours, are ideal for covering big areas and working on a large scale.

Some soft pastels are substantially softer than others. Talens' Rembrandt pastels, for instance, are fairly hard when compared with Unison and Sennelier, which are very soft. Schminke are perhaps the softest.

### Hard and soft together

Many artists find a favourite brand and stick to it. Others combine different makes, sometimes using pastels from both the main hard and soft groups; by varying the types they can achieve exact control over their paintings.

Hard and soft pastels can be used together in the same painting. It is generally easier to apply soft over hard than the other way round, simply

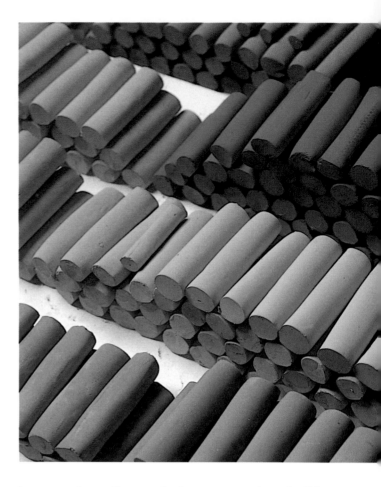

because the soft pastel pigments tend to build up on the surface of the paper, giving the harder pastels nothing to adhere to. However, if the layers of soft pastel are not too thick, it is usually quite possible to add details with harder pastels in the final stages of a painting.

### Colours

Unlike paints, pastels cannot be easily mixed. You must have a separate pastel not only for each colour but also for each different tone of that colour. This is why pastels are manufactured in such an extensive range. The manufacturer has to supply not only a viridian green, for instance, but several lighter and darker versions of it.

Some brands approach colour production in an extremely systematic way. Sennelier, for instance, include more than sixty basic colours in their extra-soft 'A l'écu' range, with between three and ten numbered shades of each colour. Unison produce their pastels in colour groups such as 'Green–Earth' and 'Red–Crimson', with eighteen harmonized colours in each group.

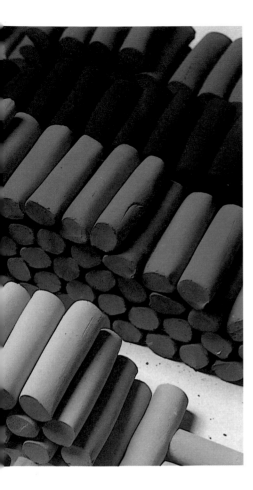

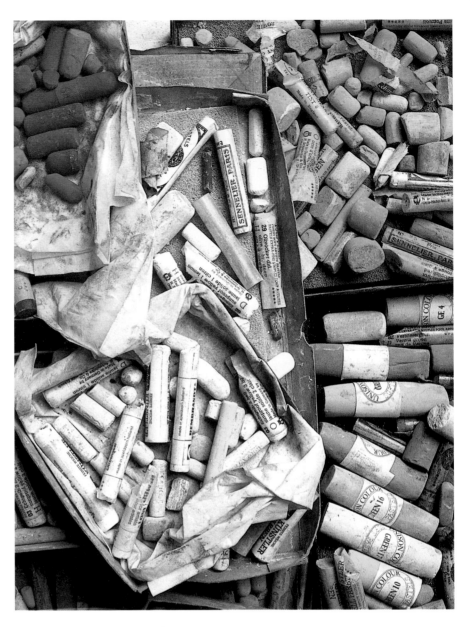

△ *Soft pastels ready to leave the factory. Several versions of each colour are manufactured.*

▷ *An assortment of soft, medium and hard pastels in the artist's studio.*

## Pastel sets

Pastels are usually sold individually, but some manufacturers also sell boxes or sets of selected colours of twelve or more. Some of these are the basic pigment colours – cadmium red, cadmium yellow, ultramarine blue, and so on. Others are selected to suit particular subjects, such as landscapes or portraits.

The sets are undoubtedly useful as an introduction to the medium, perhaps as presents. Choice of colour, however, becomes very personal; no one set will cover all the needs of an artist. A small basic set will not include enough lights and darks of any one colour to be really useful; a specialist landscape or portrait set can offer only a limited selection of someone else's choice.

If you do start off with a set, the bigger the better because the choice is greater. Even so, it will probably not be long before you want to supplement this with individual colours and tones of your own choice.

## Pastel pencils

For finer, linear work, you can also buy pastels in pencil form. These may be used on their own or – and this is what many pastel artists do – for the initial drawing stage and for adding final detail to soft pastel paintings. Carb-Othello and Conté are both well-known makers of pastel pencils and they are available in a wide range of colours.

# PASTELS BEING MADE

This book concentrates on the use rather than the making of pastels, but that process is nevertheless a fascinating one. The briefest introduction to it will help you use your pastels with deeper understanding.

Soft pastels are made by mixing pigments with a binder such as gum, resin or starch, and then rolling the mixture into sticks and leaving them to dry. The more binder used, the harder the pastel will be. Pale shades are obtained by adding varying amounts of chalk or white pigment to this basic mixture.

## Pigments

The pigments used in pastel-making are exactly the same as those found in watercolour, oil paint, acrylic and other artists' materials. The difference is that pastels require only enough binder to hold the pigment particles together, whereas with paints the pigment is usually suspended in a liquid or viscous binding solution.

Only the best pigments are used in quality pastels. These come in powder form and are obtained from many sources. Some, such as the earth colours – the umbers, siennas and ochres – are natural pigments, dug up from the ground. Others, like the madder colours, were originally vegetable extracts. Many more, including the cadmium, chrome and cobalt colours, have a mineral or chemical base, and are comparatively recent additions to the artist's palette.

## Professional pastel-making

Quality pastel-making is an extremely skilled business and the pastels are manufactured from the finest pigments, as shown in these pictures from the Unison pastel-makers in England.

Pigments vary enormously and no two colours can be made in the same way. For instance, different pigments require different binders, or combinations of binders. They also require different drying times during the manufacturing

process, so there can be no standard procedure.

Cadmium red, for example, needs a fairly strong binder; some of the earth colours, such as the umbers and siennas, hold together with a much weaker binder. With the paler shades, the chalk itself has a binding capacity, and these shades normally require only a very weak binding agent. Skimmed milk is sometimes used to bind the pale shades.

◁ 1 *Pastels are made from the same pigments as watercolours, oil paints and other artists' colours. These pigments are delivered in powder form. Depending on the colour to be made, their origins will be mineral, chemical, earth, vegetable or animal.*

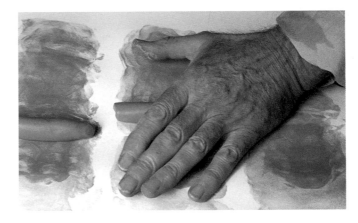

▽ 2 *At the Unison factory, pastels are handmade to the company's own special formulae. Each pigment is ground and mixed with binder, which may be gum, starch or resin, or a combination of these. Pigment properties vary considerably and each requires a different binder recipe. The mixture is then blended to a thick, buttery consistency and spooned out in equal portions on to sheets of absorbent paper.*

△ 3 *The pigment mixtures are left until excess moisture has been absorbed by the paper and the mixture is dry enough to roll. This drying time varies from pigment to pigment but can take from a few minutes to several hours. Each pastel is rolled individually by hand.*

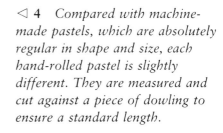

◁ 4 *Compared with machine-made pastels, which are absolutely regular in shape and size, each hand-rolled pastel is slightly different. They are measured and cut against a piece of dowling to ensure a standard length.*

▽ 5 *Each pastel is hand-finished and the cut edge smoothed off on a piece of very fine sandpaper before being packed in a foam-lined box for distribution to art-supply shops.*

19

# CARE OF PASTELS

Pastels are fragile. Press too enthusiastically with a pastel stick or drop one on a hard floor and it could easily break. Very soft pastels have so little binder that they will certainly not survive crushing or dropping. To get the best from your pastels, they should be treated with respect, handled with care and well looked after.

### A working system

It is a good idea to separate pastels into colour groups and to keep each group in a separate box or tray. A system of this sort will mean you always know exactly where to find a particular colour when you want it.

A prolific pastel artist can collect hundreds, if not thousands, of different pastels. Only a small percentage of these will be in use at any one time, because you will normally use a limited number of colours in any one painting. Rather than putting these back in the main tray each time, put the pastels currently being used in a separate box. This way the pastels you want are close at hand, and you will not have to rummage around every time you change from one colour to another.

If you are using only a few pastels, you might find it easier to hold these in a tissue as you work. When the painting is finished, the pastels can be sorted and put back in the main colour trays ready for further use.

The piles and trays of separated colours that we frequently see in the artist's studio may look beautiful, but they are purely functional. The colourful arrangements are the result of this necessary and systematic way of working.

### Cleaning pastels

A pile of much-used pastels will get dirty quickly because the pigments rub off on each other. Before long, every colour has the same homogeneous grey look. Not only does this spoil the colours in the painting; it can also make it quite difficult to tell one pastel stick from another.

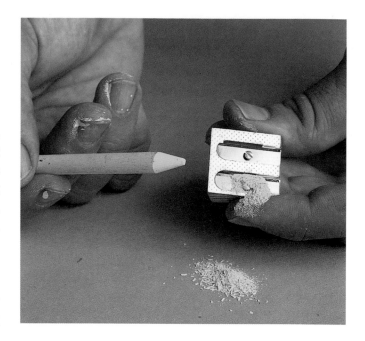

**Sharpening pastels**

△ *A reasonably hard pastel can be sharpened with an ordinary pencil sharpener. For most pastels, you will need a large sharpener.*

▽ *Hard, rectangular sticks are trickier, but if held firmly can also be sharpened with a standard pencil sharpener.*

An efficient and easy way of avoiding this is to fill the storage trays with grains of dry rice. This way, the rice gets dirty but the pastels stay clean.

## Sharpening

A pastel can be sharpened with a knife, a sharpener or sandpaper, depending on the size and softness of the stick.

Some artists, however, never sharpen pastels, preferring to draw and paint detail with a broken stick rather than with a sharpened point. By snapping a pastel in two you will get a jagged edge that can be used for lines and fine detail. However, the broken edge eventually wears smooth, and there is a limit to the number of times you can break a pastel before the pieces become too small to use.

## Fixing

Pastels are notoriously liable to smudging. The softer the stick, the greater the risk, but even hard pastels will smudge if you accidentally touch or rub the picture as you work.

The only way to prevent this is to use fixative, a liquid spray that works rather like hair spray. This is available from art shops, usually in spray cans. Alternatively, you can buy it in bottles and apply it with a diffuser. Either use the fixative as you work, fixing each stage of the painting to stop smudging as the picture progresses, or simply fix the completed picture.

Fixative is actually a varnish, and too much will seal the pastel surface, making it difficult to work. It also darkens the colours, and should therefore be applied sparingly.

▷ *A sharp scalpel or craft knife is a useful sharpening tool, but the softer sticks crumble and break easily, so this must be done with great care.*

▷ ▽ *For maintaining a point as you work, keep a sheet of sandpaper nearby. Turn the pastel gently as you rub, to get an even point.*

# SURFACES

The right sort of surface is crucial to the pastel artist. There are a lot to choose from.

To start with, buy boards or papers which are specially made for pastel work. These have a definite texture, or tooth, which holds the pastel dust and allows you to build up the colours in a way not possible on smoother surfaces. Avoid the temptation to 'practise' on cheap, white paper because the result will look so awful that you will be quickly disheartened.

## Tooth

The tiny indents in any textured surface are known as the 'tooth'. If you work on a surface with no tooth, your pastels will slide around and you will get skid marks instead of the rich matt effect normally associated with pastel painting. On the right surface, however, your pastel colour will fill the holes gradually, enabling you to build up several layers of pastel before the indented surface is unable to take any more.

You will know when your support has reached its limit because it gets more difficult to make the colours adhere. Test this by gently tapping the back of your painting. If you have reached your limit, tiny flakes and particles will drop off.

If this does happen before you have finished working, you can rescue the built-up areas by brushing with a stiff brush or scraping some of the pigment off with the flat side of a scalpel blade.

## Papers and boards

So many pastel supports are now available that it is not very helpful merely to list and describe them. They are all different – some coarse, others velvety, and so on – and the only way to find out what suits you is to try a few. The Fabriano and Canson Mi-Teintes papers are among the most popular. Both come in a good range of colours.

Pastel boards have the same surface textures as papers but are rigid, which is particularly useful if you are combining pastel with paint or water, because boards will not buckle.

*(Left to right) Fabriano, Velour, Ingres, Canson, Fabriano.*

## Other supports

Velour papers have a velvety surface, and sanded papers are gritty. Both can produce beautifully rich effects and are well worth trying. The sanded papers wear down the pastels considerably quicker than standard surfaces, especially if you use very soft sticks. Sanded papers should not be used with water or water-based paints, as water can dissolve the adhesive which keeps the particles of sand in place.

An inexpensive alternative to the sanded papers sold in art shops is very fine sandpaper, or flour paper, which can be bought in hardware and tool shops. The use of these commercial sandpapers is widespread and very practical, although it should be said that they are not made from acid-free materials like the art papers, and pastel colours could possibly deteriorate with time.

Another, rather unusual, pastel surface is marble-dust board. This sounds very gritty and coarse, but actually has a mild, velvety texture which holds the pigment well. These boards can be difficult to find in art shops, but you can make your own quite easily (instructions for doing this are on page 26).

Other suitable surfaces are canvas- or muslin-covered pastel boards, which have a fine fabric veneer. Although they are not at all difficult to use, they produce a very distinctive surface texture. On the whole, it is wiser to try these only when you have had some experience of more conventional surfaces. Again, soft pastel sticks can disappear alarmingly quickly as they are dragged across the textured surface.

# TINTING WITH PAINT

Most pastel papers come in such a good selection of colours that you rarely need to tint them. However, there will be times when you do not have exactly the right coloured support for the subject you want to paint. In these cases, it is an easy job to give the surface of the support a coat of colour mixed to your own individual requirement. Other types of support – canvas boards and marble-dust boards, for instance – are not available in the same extensive choice of colours as the papers, and in these instances you may well need to tint your own.

You can use any type of paint, or a pastel wash, for your tint, but the surface must be strong enough to withstand the moisture without buckling. Boards and rigid supports are fine, but papers can sometimes wrinkle if you do not mount or stretch them first.

### Acrylic

For a solid, opaque tint that does not dissolve in water or other liquids, use acrylic paint. If your board has a 'toothy' surface, simply mix the colour you want and paint it on with broad strokes to get a flat colour. If the board is not 'toothy', acrylic gesso mixed with the paint will give your surface

△ 2 *Pour the tinted mixture into the basic solution and stir well. If the tint is dark enough, repeat this until you have the required colour. Do not attempt to squeeze the paint directly into the gesso solution, otherwise you will get lumps of uneven colour on the support.*

### Tinting with paint

▷ 1 *Mix the acrylic gesso with enough water for the solution to be easily painted on to your support. To tint the ground, pour a little of this solution into a smaller, separate container and mix well with acrylic paint until you have the colour and tone you require. (Note: Acrylic gesso is a viscous substance, available in jars from your art shop. It is not to be confused with traditional gesso, which is completely different and comes in powder form.)*

enough of a texture to receive the pastels.

Depending on the thickness of the colour, the acrylic tint will dry in just a few minutes; the process can be speeded up by using a hairdryer.

## Oil

For sanded papers, use oil paints diluted with turpentine instead of acrylics. In this context, oils are better for two reasons: sanded papers are less likely to buckle with oils; and the oil-based colours will not disturb the sandy texture of the paper.

Oil paint is much slower-drying than acrylic, so allow for this; keep the colour thin by mixing with turpentine or white spirits. Even so, remember that oil paint normally takes a few days to dry. Therefore you should do your tinting well in advance.

The diluted colours will give you a wash rather than an opaque covering, so if you want an even colour apply the paint in broad, horizontal stripes across the paper. For an irregular effect, apply the paint in criss-cross strokes.

△ **3** *Use a clean, flat-bristled brush and apply the gesso to the paper or card. You may need two or even three coats to get a completely flat colour.*

# MAKING A MARBLE-DUST BOARD

Marble dust, which looks rather like talcum powder, can be bought in many art shops. It is an inert substance – in other words, it will not deteriorate with age – so any that is left over can be kept for future use.

To make it stick on to the surface of the support, marble dust must be mixed with an adhesive binder, such as acrylic gesso. If it is used on its own, gesso produces a good but fine pastel surface; the marble dust gives it extra tooth, and a nice irregular finish. Yet the dust is fine and powdery rather than gritty, so the finished surface will be quite velvety to the touch.

**Surface texture**

The quantities used here produced a thin, milky liquid which was then applied in several layers to build up a tough, opaque ground. The more layers you apply, the more textured the surface becomes.

It is unwise to take short-cuts by adding too much dust to the gesso, because if the mixture becomes too thick the brushstrokes will stand out and spoil the surface. It must be built up in several thin coats, allowing each coat to dry thoroughly before applying the next.

**Making a marble-dust board**

◁ 1 *You will need board, acrylic gesso, marble dust (available from art shops), water, a container for mixing, a manual egg-beater and a brush.*

▽ 2 *Pour about half a litre of gesso into the container – less if you need only a small quantity. Add a little water, enough to get a creamy consistency which is easy to apply to the board.*

◁ 3   To half a litre of acrylic gesso, add about a dessertspoonful of marble dust. Increase this quantity if you want a particularly coarse surface for your pastels.

▽ 4   Whisk the mixture with the egg-beater until it is smooth and creamy. If you want to tint the board, do this now with acrylic paint (see pages 24–5).

△ 5   Paint the board in criss-cross brushstrokes to get an even finish.

▽ 6   A second and, if possible, a third coat of the gesso solution will give you a completely opaque pastel surface.

# LAYING A PASTEL TINT

A pastel wash, the simplest of all tinting methods, can be applied in seconds to give a single- or multicoloured background to your painting.

With this method you have absolute control, but you should plan a little in advance. If you are thinking of a particular subject and want to vary the colour of the ground for certain parts of the painting, you should take this factor into consideration during the tinting stage.

For a landscape subject, for instance, you might want the sky area to be one colour and the rest of the paper to be another. In this case it would be simply a matter of blocking in those areas with the appropriate coloured pastels.

**Pastel wash**
When you have applied your background in this way, you should stop to consider two possible alternatives which can make quite a difference to the next stages. You can leave the pastel background as it is with a dry, grainy texture; or you can dissolve it with water or turpentine to create a very lively, loose wash on which to start your pastel painting.

### Dissolving a pastel tint

◁ **1** *For a washy effect, apply a thin layer of pastel with the side of the stick.*

▽ **2** *Using a large brush, spread the colour across the support. Here the artist is using irregular strokes to create an uneven colour; horizontal strokes will produce a more even effect.*

### Laying a pastel tint

◁ **1** *To get an overall pastel tone before drawing the subject, completely cover the support with colour, using the side of the stick.*

▷ **2** *Brush the colour with a soft, clean brush – this will spread the pastel evenly without clogging the support.*

▷, ▷ **3** *For a darker tone, apply more pastel colour and blend with the soft brush. If required, you can use another colour for this and subsequent layers.*

29

# SECURING THE SURFACE

Pastel papers, which are available in an ever-increasing range of colours these days, are also relatively inexpensive – certainly when compared with boards and other rigid supports. Moreover, the paper is usually heavy and of good quality.

Despite these advantages, however, you should not forget that any sheet of paper is always more vulnerable and more difficult to work on than a rigid support. Some preparation, therefore, is advisable.

### Mounting

There are various ways of strengthening the support. The first is simply to mount your paper before starting work. If you glue the sheet on to a stiff card, you will not need a drawing board, because the support can be placed directly on the easel. A mounted sheet is also better able to tolerate wetting, so it can be used with paint and other liquids without buckling.

Ideally, you should use acid-free board or card for the backing, because this does not deteriorate with age. The impurities in ordinary cardboard can affect the pastel colours over a period of time.

An alternative, equally easy, precaution is to fix the paper to a stiff card with masking tape. This method is completely reversible. When the painting is finished, you can remove it from its backing by cutting it out with a ruler and scalpel.

### Padding paper

If you do decide to work directly on to the paper without mounting, it is a good idea to place one or two sheets of cheap paper under your pastel paper – especially if you are working on a hard wooden drawing board, where the surface texture of the wood can show through in the pastel marks. These extra sheets cushion the support, giving you a softer, more receptive pastel surface.

Make sure the padding sheets are the same size or larger than the pastel paper; otherwise the edges will show up as ugly ridges in the painting.

**Mounting paper**
◁ 1  You will need pastel paper, stiff mounting card and spray adhesive.

▷ 2  Spray the reverse side of the paper with the adhesive, keeping the spray well away from the mounting board and other materials.

▽ 3  Position the paper on the mounting board, adhesive side down, and press firmly outwards from the centre.

**Using tape**
△ 1  You will need paper, a sheet of mounting card and masking tape.

▽ 2  Place the paper centrally on the board, cut the tape to the four lengths of the paper and press firmly.

**Padding**
▽ For a smooth, cushioned pastel surface, place two or more sheets of paper under the pastel paper before starting work. The underpapers should be the same size or larger than the pastel support.

# ERASING AND FIXING

### Erasing

There is no such thing as an irreversible mistake with pastels. They are a forgiving medium, and mistakes can usually be erased or rubbed back to the support. A soft, kneadable eraser is best because the harder ones tend to break up into tiny flakes, which then get rubbed into the pastel pigment and can be difficult to remove without smudging the painting. A kneadable eraser, however, remains intact and can be moulded to a point to erase the tiniest mistakes with great precision.

White bread is a popular alternative, but suitable only for larger areas. It leaves a surprisingly clean surface, and you simply blow away the crumbs when you have finished. Pastel artists who use this method point out that the bread must be white; wholemeal bread does not work!

Other accessible alternatives are tissue, cloth, kitchen towel or a stiff brush. Brushes are particularly useful for clearing a support that has become clogged up before you have finished working on it. Because the stiff bristles are abrasive, they loosen unwanted pigment particles without flattening the surface.

### Fixative

Whether to use fixative or not is a question that always seems to cause argument. Some artists use it a lot – after every stage of a painting and then, finally, to fix the finished pictures. There are others who refuse to use fixative at all. They claim that it darkens the colours – which is true – and that this can change the tonal values of a composition. Then again there are some artists who use fixative for precisely this darkening effect.

As a general guide, however, it is a good idea to fix a finished pastel painting, simply because it will be extremely fragile if you do not. An accidental brush with an unfixed painting can spoil hours of work in a second.

### Spray with care

Use the fixative sparingly, holding the can or diffuser a foot or so away from the vertical painting and moving the spray slowly from side to side to cover the painting in horizontal strokes. Practise on a blank sheet of paper first; it is very easy to swamp your painting, or even to cause runs of fixative which stain the painting.

It should also be remembered that fixative is a varnish and seals the pastel pigments in position. If it is overused as you work, it will eventually build up and produce a shiny, hard surface that rejects further pastel colour. The pastel stick then merely slides around without making a mark.

To some extent pastels will fix naturally if left alone in a safe place. Pinning them to the wall in a position where they will not be brushed against is one solution. Another is to store them in a plan chest.

◁ **Kneadable eraser**
*A kneadable eraser will remove pastel marks, taking you back to the paper. To erase small areas, mould the eraser into a fine point.*

▷ **Bread**
*White bread can be used to erase large areas of pastel and will leave you with a suprisingly clean surface.*

▽ *A clean stiff brush is useful for removing pastel pigment from specific areas where you want to apply more pastel. Here the artist is removing part of the thick background colour where she intends to paint flower heads.*

# A PLACE TO WORK

The ideal artist's studio has plenty of light and space and a large north-facing window. The trouble is, however, that most of us have to work in rooms that fall far short of these optimum conditions. A little ingenuity is usually needed to make the most of the space available.

### Space and furniture

No matter how small your workspace, try to lay it out so that you can walk around easily without bumping into things. Also, try to arrange the room so that you can stand back from your painting. Composition and colour values can be properly assessed only if you stand away and view your painting from a reasonable distance.

Whether you work standing up or sitting down, a table or worktop should be close at hand for pastels, tissues and other materials. The pastels themselves always take up a lot of space, and it is much easier to organize the colours if you have a sizeable surface on which to lay out and separate the various ranges and tones.

A sturdy, upright easel is almost essential, certainly if you prefer to stand at your work. If you are sitting, a pile of books can serve as a temporary substitute, but the support inevitably moves around and eventually you will want a more permanent solution. Unless you like to work on a very large scale, a wooden table easel could be the answer – this is especially useful in a confined space.

When planning your studio space, allow room for storage. This is particularly important to the pastel artist; the finished paintings are vulnerable and must be kept somewhere out of harm's way where they are not going to get smudged. A plan chest is good because it has wide drawers and protects the pictures from dust. They should be stored between sheets of protective paper to prevent the pictures from rubbing together. For stacking rigid supports and framed paintings, a simple wooden rack is useful and easy to make.

### Lighting

Good natural lighting is a great advantage to the pastel artist, whose main concern is with the effects of light and colour. Because daylight is naturally unstable, changing not only with the weather but also gradually throughout the day, this can cause problems. If you start painting a still life in brilliant sunshine, the shadows and colours will alter completely if the sun goes in.

The problem is even more pronounced if you have a south-facing window. In this case, the light is more direct and casts stark, hard shadows. A white muslin or cotton curtain across the window is often helpful, because it allows the light to enter but also softens the harshness.

problems, but with a horizontal support you should be more careful. Try not to lean directly over the painting or to work too close to the support; otherwise you are likely to breath in pigment particles. Regular users of soft pastels sometimes wear a mask to eliminate this risk. Pastel dust gathers rapidly, especially on the floor around the easel, so use a vacuum cleaner regularly to keep it to a minimum.

Fixative is another studio material that should not be inhaled. Apart from being potentially harmful, it has a strong smell, so follow the manufacturers' instructions and use it only in a well-ventilated room.

◁ *Artist Charmian Edgerton at work in her studio. Pastels and other materials are arranged on a spacious tabletop close to hand, and she works at a drawing board supported by a sturdy, adjustable easel.*

▽ *This useful pastel tray is postioned in front of the easel, enabling the artist to work and select colours without having to change position.*

Many artists prefer artificial light to the uncertainty of daylight. Some use a combination of the two, so that when the natural light disappears there is another, stable, source of light to work from.

### Safety

Pastels and other artists' materials are now manufactured to strict safety regulations, with certain toxic pigments banned and others allowed only in small, safe quantities. Even so, soft pastels inevitably produce a lot of dust, and you should take sensible precautions to avoid inhaling this.

If you work with the support upright, most of the dust will fall to the floor without causing

# Colour in pastels

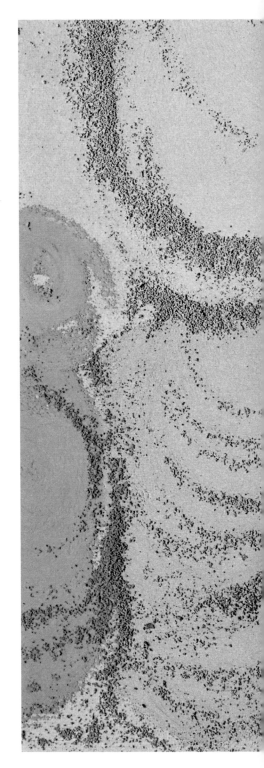

Even though many colours in pastel come ready-made, the pastel painter still needs a thorough understanding of colour and its effects. Pastel artists have certain ways of mixing colour in the painting itself. For instance, by working in dots and dashes of blue and red, you can create the impression of violet. The blues and reds will combine in the eye of the viewer to create a particular colour illusion. This, in fact, is the principle that was followed by the Impressionists, who felt that the colours of nature were not mixed as on a palette but shone individually in a way which mingled in the viewer's eye. This is why their pictures – some of them done with pastels – have that distinctive shimmering and glowing effect.

With hundreds of colours to choose from, you will need advice about where to start. This chapter contains suggestions, for instance, on how to select one or two light and dark versions of various colours, so that you can go forward from there.

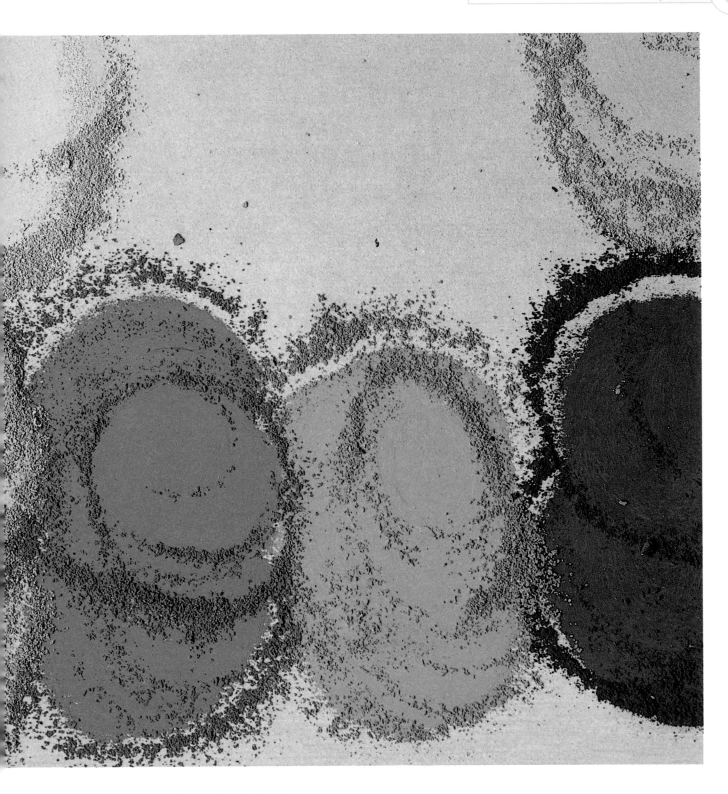

*Choosing your pastel colours should be a joy, not a chore. When next confronted by a bewildering array in the art shop, remember that the manufacturer is on your side. Pastels are not paints and most of the mixing is done in the factory, not on your palette. We suggest a basic general selection of colours to start you off. It will not be long before you find your own personal colour range.*

# CREATING COLOUR

If you had a paintbox containing just red, yellow and blue, in theory you could mix any other colour you wanted. For these three are the 'primary colours', and from then come the 'secondary colours' – orange, green and violet – and then the 'tertiary colours' – yellowy green, bluish green, yellowy orange and so on.

With pastels, you cannot mix these – or any other – colours as easily, so each one has to be manufactured and sold as a separate stick. Nor can you mix lighter and darker versions of a colour by adding black or white, so each colour has to be sold in a range of lights and darks, or tones.

The resulting ranges of tone and colour seem enormous – some manufacturers have a range of more than 500 pastels. But the choice becomes much less daunting once you realize the need for such a large selection, and once you understand that the manufacturer is actually doing your colour-mixing for you, making your job easier.

## Warm and cools

The warm colours are reds, yellows, oranges and earthy browns – colours associated with the sun and heat. Cool colours are greens, blues and violets. When you hear an artist speak of a 'warm' green, this means a green which contains a lot of warm yellow or a touch of red. A 'cold' red is a bluish red, such as crimson – red that contains a lot of blue.

Warms and cools are important to all artists, because without a balance between the two a painting lacks interest and resonance. They are especially important to pastel artists, because their frequency of use in a subject often determines the choice of paper colour.

A landscape or sea painting which contains lots of blues and greens is usually more effective when done on a warm-toned paper, for instance. This is because the contrasting background colours show up between the pastel colours, making them look

particularly effective and resonant. (There is more about paper colour on page 46.)

## A basic palette

An initial colour selection based loosely on the wheel below would be a good starting point. The bright colours should therefore include a cadmium red, cadmium orange and alizarin crimson; a

*Primary colours are red, yellow and blue; the secondary colours are orange, green and violet. This pastel colour wheel shows pale and dark tones of each colour.*

reddish violet and a bluish violet; viridian green and a yellowish green; cerulean, cobalt and ultramarine blue; and cadmium and lemon yellow.

You should then aim to acquire some 'neutral' or grey versions of those same colours – some dull yellows, grey-greens, grey-blues and so on.

You will also need some light and dark versions of each of the colour-wheel pastels, for shadows and highlights. Until you know your needs and discover your preferences, two tones of each of these colours is enough to start with – a very deep and a very pale one. Many manufacturers produce their colours in numbered ranges; thus Cadmium Red 0 would be very pale pink and Cadmium Red 9 a very deep red.

Pastels can be bought individually or in sets. The Unison sets shown here each contain a broad variety of pastels from a single colour group; a general-purpose set normally includes a comprehensive range of all the basic colours. The red range (right) includes autumnal and earth reds, pinks, oranges, reddish-purple and primary red.

Essential for the landscape artist, this selection of green includes muted olives, bright blue-green and lime.

*Blues range from neutral greyish-blues to warm violet and cool cobalt.*

# The basics

NOW COMES that awesome moment when you face an empty sheet of paper. Because many people find it difficult to get going on a picture, we have asked one of our artists to demonstrate eight possible ways of starting a painting, using the same subject. The aim of this exercise is to demystify the process of pastel painting by showing that there is no one right way of working. The beginner is all too often confronted with a finished product – a daunting experience if you have not been shown how the work began.

After looking at the demonstrations here, why not carry out a similar experiment of your own, bearing in mind that you are not restricted to just one approach.

In this chapter we have also taken steps of which some purists might not approve. In some demonstrations, the artist has begun by painting the subject in very broad terms, using gouache or acrylic. The aim here is to encourage you to start out by filling the whole page rather than beginning with a few pastel strokes – something that can happen if you are over-tentative. Later, you will be advised to use pastel itself, in many cases in the same broad, bold manner as the gouache and acrylic, so that you can get your painting started with confidence.

Bold shapes of colour are set off by
the dark tone of the paper in these
decorative flower-painting details.
The importance of background
tone, along with simple pastel
techniques and other basics of
pastel painting, are covered in the
following pages.

## TECHNIQUES

# PASTEL MARKS

The marks made by pastels depend largely on what sort of pastel you are using – hard or soft, chunky or fine. Many people assume a soft pastel is more difficult to use than a harder one simply because it is more crumbly. Certainly soft pastels do crumble easily and can produce messy dust. But a soft pastel is actually more flexible and can give a wider range of marks.

With a soft pastel you can build up thick colour quickly and cover large areas easily. By breaking the pastel stick and using the broken edge, you can produce a line as fine as any made by a sharp pencil. Some extremely soft pastels can be unwieldy – especially the giant ones which are used mainly for chunky marks and large areas.

Harder pastels last longer and are easier to control, being less likely to smudge. Some are rectangular, making them excellent for drawing. Use any corner for a fine, precision mark. For a broad line, draw with the width of the stick.

**The drawing**
Most pastel paintings begin with a line drawing.

▷ *Sharp, precise lines are made with the jagged edge of a broken pastel. The thickness and density of a drawn line can be varied by altering the pressure on the pastel stick (top). Similar tonal variations can be created in solid areas of colour by varying the pressure on the side of the pastel stick (below).*

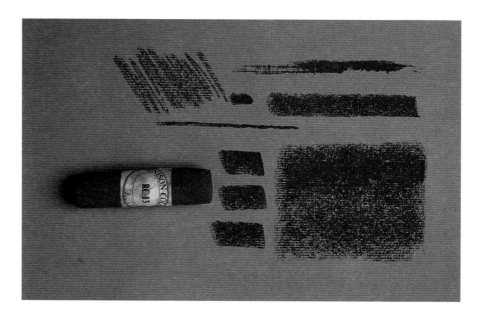

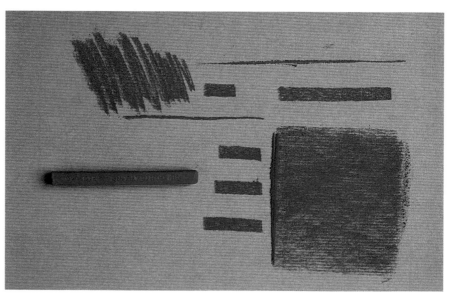

Some are extremely precise, showing every detail and every tiny shadow of the subject. More usually with pastels, the drawing is a light but accurate sketch, intended only as a basic guide for the ensuing colour. For a preliminary drawing, choose a material you feel comfortable with – you may find pencil or charcoal suits better than pastel.

A simple drawing generally makes for a less inhibited painting. If you do use pastel, then the harder varieties can be easily worked over with softer pastels later on. It is slightly more difficult to use hard pastels on top of soft ones. For drawing on a large scale, you might find it quicker and easier to draw with the whole length of the pastel – especially effective with the rectangular variety, because you can use either the sharp or flat edge, and this gives you a choice of line.

**Blocking in**
When blocking in the first solid stages of your pastel painting it is a good idea to use the entire length of the stick. This helps to cover a large area at a time, roughing in the whole composition quickly, using the approximate colour of each area. It also lets you apply colour extremely lightly, so the pigment merely catches the surface of the support. You can then change your mind and make corrections by brushing off the first colour. A thin layer of initial colour leaves the support relatively clean and unclogged for further working.

◁ *Broad areas of colour can be quickly blocked in using the side of the pastel. For a thick, heavy line, draw with the flattened end of the stick; use the edge of the flattened end for drawing fine lines. Very chunky pastels produce soft, feathery marks (top). Hard pastels (below) are less crumbly and therefore less vulnerable to smudging.*

# TONED PAPERS

Very rarely do you see a pastel painting which has been done on a completely white paper. And even on those occasions when white is used, it is usually because the artist has started with a bold underpainting which obliterated the white in the very early stages.

## Tone

There are two good reasons why pastel artists work mainly on toned or coloured papers.

The first is to do with the tone itself. Quite simply, if you start with a medium-toned paper, then you can immediately begin establishing the extreme darks and lights by relating these to the mid-tone of the paper. If you start with a white background, the first job must be to get rid of some of the bright whiteness, because it distorts the other tones. Much better to start with a toned paper in the first place and make this part of the painting.

The second concerns the subject matter. If your subject is predominantly dark with few light areas or highlights – a night scene or a shadowy interior, perhaps – then you might decide on a fairly deep-toned paper, in keeping with the mood and atmosphere of the subject. For a dark subject with areas or patches of contrasting light, it may be more effective to choose a pale paper to help you establish these contrasts.

Whatever the reasons for your choice, it is important that the decision you make is a considered one. The tone of the paper will play a crucial role in the finished picture.

## Colour

The other important factor is the actual colour of the paper, and this should make a positive contribution to the painting. As you can see from the sketches here, similar pastel colours look totally different against different backgrounds. Choose a background that complements your pastels, and the colours will sing; use one that does not, and the painting can die.

In the majority of cases, the paper colour is

visible in the finished painting. Often this is the background behind the subject; occasionally it shows up as barely discernible flecks between pastel strokes. However, even if the paper is not actually visible at all in the completed picture, when it has been totally obliterated by densely overlaid pastel, it is still vitally important and has certainly affected the painting. This is because the artist's choice of colour and tone throughout has

△ 1  *The colour contrast between the cool blue paper and the warm brown pastel ensures that the image shows up clearly.*

been determined by the colour of the paper he or she is working on.

**Warm or cool background**

Choice of background colour frequently depends on colour 'temperature' – the warms and cools in the subject. Portrait painters are particularly aware of this, and their backgrounds are often cool, deep greens or greys, chosen to complement the paler, warm tones of most flesh colours. On the other hand, if the subject's face contains a lot of cool shadows and deep tones, the background may be paler or warmer for this reason.

Similarly, many landscapes are cool greens, greys and blues. The most popular landscape papers are earthy browns, dusty oranges and warm sepias – contrasts that make the cooler colours of the landscape seem more vivid and vibrant.

◁ 3   *The horse is similar in colour and tone to the background paper, but the intensity of the bright orange pastel compensates for the overall lack of contrast.*

▽ 4   *Dark outlines and heavy shading in this drawing are emphasized by the paleness of the paper. The artist has used the tone of the paper to indicate the light areas on the horse.*

◁ 2   *Pale paper emphasizes the main outline of the moving horse. A medium tone is introduced for the lighter, subtle shading.*

TECHNIQUES

# WAYS WITH PASTEL

Look at a collection of work by different artists, and you will see just how varied pastel paintings can be.

No matter how diverse these paintings are, however, they will always closely involve tone and colour. The secret of all paintings is the successful combination of these two elements in the same picture. An apple, for instance, may be green and red, but it also has a light side and a shaded side. How to combine the local colour – the red and green – with the right amount of light and shade is what painting is all about.

For these apple paintings, the artist took a different approach for each demonstration. As you can see, there is no standard way of working so it is worth trying them all, just to see which one suits you best.

The techniques are demonstrated on a relatively simple subject in order to show clearly how the pastels are used. In your own paintings, you will probably want to combine some of these techniques while evolving your own individual way of working.

**Different approaches**
Whatever the individual methods, however, almost

▽ **Charcoal**  *Pastel and charcoal are entirely compatible, and many pastel artists use charcoal for the initial drawing. Excess charcoal can be brushed away before painting starts, leaving you with a pale outline that does not interfere with the pastel colours.*

▷ **Tonal underpainting**  *A black and white underpainting can act as a guide to the tones of an object when you start working in colour. Again, brush away excess black dust before applying colour.*

every artist starts by establishing the colour or tonal values – or combination of both – in a very general way before developing the painting. You can do this by looking at your subject and deciding on the main areas of colour, and where these are affected by light and shadow. Choose the pastels you need to establish these areas, then lightly block them in.

To pick out these main areas, it is helpful to half close your eyes so that the subject becomes slightly out of focus. By limiting your vision in this way,

you will be able to see only the main, relevant areas, cutting out distracting details.

**Tone first**
You might find it easier to get the tones right – the lights and darks – before tackling the colour. You can do this by making a fairly precise black and white underdrawing, which can then be worked into with colours of the appropriate tone. Alternatively, it may be sufficient to roughly block in the dark areas as you make your initial outline drawing – just to guide you as to where the shadows go.

If you do go for a 'tone first' approach, it is best to fix the black and white before overlaying any colour, or to brush away excess dust; otherwise the underpainting will mix with the pastel colours, which will turn muddy.

▽ **Painted undercolour** *Beginning with the local or real colours of the subject is a classic start for pastel paintings. Gouache or acrylic paint will give you a solid base of colour, to which you can add shadows, highlights and reflections.*

△ **Broad areas of colour** *By using the length of the stick to establish the subject in the first stages of a painting, you will get a lively, broad underpainting which can then be developed in more detail.*

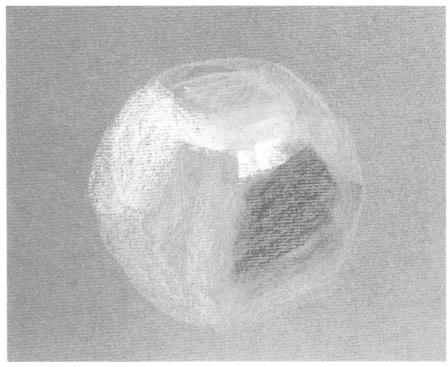

▷ **Working from light to dark** *Starting with the palest colours enables you to build up the darker tones gradually. A word of caution, however: it is quite difficult to get extremely dark tones with soft pastel, especially when working over pale ones, so if your subject is tonally very dark, you would be wise to avoid starting with the palest colours.*

◁ **Working from dark to light** *It is much easier for the pastel artist to get a good, solid pale tone than it is to achieve a very dark one. For this reason pastels are traditionally used mainly – though by no means always – from dark to light. Here the artist has started with some of the deeper colours, into which the lights and highlights can be worked.*

▷ **Erasing** *The artist started painting this apple in solid blocks of pastel colour, then used a kneadable eraser to work back to the neutral tone of the paper in certain areas. The erased areas can either be left as they are or developed at a later stage.*

◁ **Cross-hatching** *A cross-hatched underpainting is an unusual way of starting a painting, but it can be a useful guide for subsequent areas of more solid colour. It is quite easy to apply a soft pastel over a harder one, so do the cross-hatching in fairly hard pastels. This will allow plenty of scope for development with softer colour.*

TECHNIQUES

# BLENDING

One way to mix pastel colours is to rub them together on the paper. You can do this with all types of pastel, although the softer and more crumbly they are, the more easily they can be rubbed and blended.

These demonstrations show pastels being blended with finger, brush, tissue and torchon. The torchon is best used in small areas. It is especially good for corners and sharp shapes. For the large areas and backgrounds, however, all the other methods are quicker and equally good.

A soft brush will produce softly blended colour, but a stiff brush, such as the oil-painting brush being used here, will remove more pigment, and you have to be careful not to take away more colour than you intended. Persistent rubbing with a stiff brush will actually remove most of the pastel and the brush is sometimes used as an eraser for that reason.

### When to blend
Blending produces a very smooth-looking surface. It is especially useful if you want to capture in your painting the essence of a particular smooth or shiny object in the subject. Porcelain, glass, water and skin are just a few of the surfaces on which you might want to use blended colour.

**Finger blending** *The quickest and most instinctive way of blending pastel colours is to rub them together with your finger.*

**The torchon** *Torchons are available from any art shop. The pointed tip of the torchon enables you to blend small, precise areas of colour.*

The blending technique is also useful if you have two adjoining colours and want to smooth them together to achieve a gradual colour transition. In this case, the blended area will turn into a third colour – a mixture of the two main areas. Thus the transition from red to yellow is orange; blue to red, violet; and so on.

Similarly, two overlaid colours can be blended to create a solid third colour. If you apply a thin layer of yellow over red, for example, the general effect will be orange; but because pastel is applied in dry strokes, you will also be able to see the orange and red marks. By blending the colours together, however, you will get an area of solid orange.

### When to stop

The negative side to the blending process is that it can easily be overdone, and is best used selectively. There is a tendency among newcomers to pastels to blend colours, because they feel this produces a more 'realistic' picture, possibly because blending can make a painting look like a photograph. However, the opposite is usually true, and it is always a mistake to use blending in an attempt to rescue or disguise a weak drawing.

Overblending can destroy the form it is trying to describe by making the subject look flat and two-dimensional. The result tends to be a bland painting with everything in it looking as if it is made of rubber. Careful observation of the subject, combined with good drawing and painting, is far more important, and you can actually make an accurate and realistic painting without any blending at all.

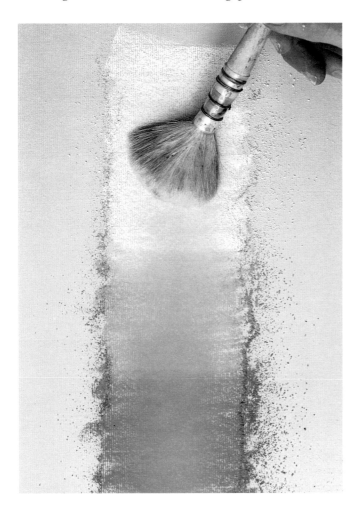

**Using a soft brush**  *Any soft-bristled brush can be used for blending pastels. Stiffer bristles are too abrasive and will remove the pigment particles altogether.*

**Tissues and cloth**  *For blending and smoothing larger areas of colour, you can use cloth, paper tissue or kitchen towel.*

# TECHNIQUES

# STILL LIFE USING TONE

### Working in monochrome

Before embarking on a complicated subject – one in which you have to contend with many different colours as well as the various tones of each of those colours – try doing a picture in monochrome. This means either using black, white and grey, as the artist does here, or, if you happen to have several pastel tones of a particular colour, using these with black and white.

### Using tone

When using paints rather than pastels, you can mix different tones of a colour by adding varying amounts of black or white. If you have three tubes of paint – say, black, white and red – you can mix the darkest red and palest pink, as well as all the tones in between, from the three basics.

With pastels, the process is slightly different because you have to apply the tones separately. You therefore need a different pastel for each tone you are using. So you would need not only red, black and white pastels but also a stick of pale pink, one of dark red and as many in-between tones as necessary.

Once you get used to the idea of separate tones, it is actually much easier than mixing a lighter or darker colour each time you need it, as you would have to do with paints. As each new tone is introduced into your pastel picture, you can lay the stick aside, ready for further use.

### Tinted paper

It will make things much easier if you start with tinted or coloured paper, because the light and dark tones will show up against this. Your paper effectively becomes a medium tone, enabling you to start straight away by putting in the very lightest and the very darkest areas.

▷ **1** *The subject is colourful, with lots of contrasting tones – lights and darks. Obvious darks are the black checks in the cloth and the shadows; the palest tones are the white checks and the highlights on the fruit. Other colours lie somewhere between these extremes, and must be indicated in an appropriate shade of grey. When looking for the right grey, you may find it helpful to imagine how a particular colour would look in a black and white photograph.*

▽ **2** *There were twelve tones in the artist's pastel selection, including black and white, but you can easily use less. A dark, medium and light grey with black and white, for example, will give you ample scope if you simplify the tones.*

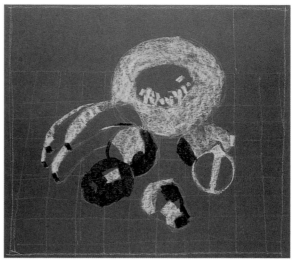

△ 4 *A few of the darker local colours and shadows are added in black and deep grey. At this stage, each area of tone is simplified into a solid block. The shadow on the orange is just a single wedge of black, with no attempt made to blend it to indicate the roundness of the fruit.*

▽ 3 *Choose a mid-grey paper, because this can initially be used as a medium tone and will help you to establish the lights and darks in the early stages. Here, the artist has started by blocking in some of the very lightest tones with the white pastel.*

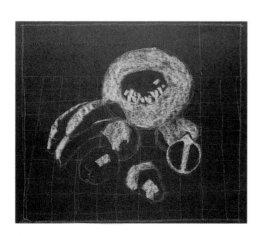

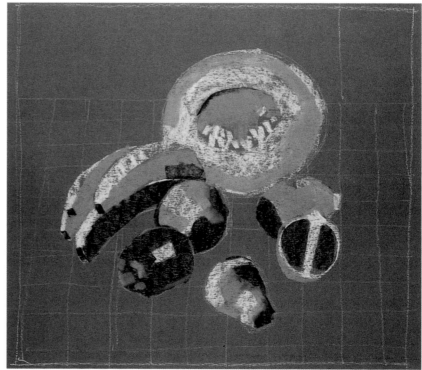

△ 5 *The tones already laid act as a guide for further lights and darks. The artist can use the new tones to describe the various shapes and forms within the still life. For instance, a mid-grey has been worked into the pear. This medium tone represents the local colour of the fruit and, by relating this to the dark shadow and the highlight which have already been established, the pear becomes a solid, rounded form.*

▷ 8   *The denseness of the white in the tablecloth causes other tones in the still life to appear rather weak in comparison. The artist works back into the painting, developing and adjusting these tones to bring them into line with the strong white of the cloth.*

△ 6   *Black and dark grey are used to block in the checks of the tablecloth. The cloth provides a definite base for the still-life arrangement. Instead of floating against a flat grey background, the fruit is now given a spatial context; there is suggested space behind and in front of the fruit.*

▽ 7   *The bright white tablecloth checks are added. The artist simplifies the cloth by ignoring the subtle changes of light across the table surface. Each check is blocked in as a flat tone – black, white or dark grey. The slightly receding lines of the pattern help to give a sense of space to the composition.*

▽ 9 *Finally, the artist blocks in the darkest portion of background. Again, this addition alters the tonal values elsewhere in the picture, making it necessary to slightly readjust and define some of the tones.*

# TECHNIQUES

# PAINT AND WATER

Making the first marks can be the most frightening step of all, yet this is exactly the moment when you need to feel most confident.

At the start of a painting, unfamiliar subjects are naturally approached with caution and new materials with respect. Most of us have a fairly realistic idea of our own limitations and avoid embarking on projects we feel are outside our abilities. (This cautious approach is one that comes with experience and will probably save you from many disappointments.)

Sadly, this same caution can also prevent us from trying new ideas and thus possibly from producing our best work.

More than any other art medium, pastels respond well to confident handling and bold experiments. They can also be profoundly dull when used over-cautiously. Held tentatively, pastels produce feeble, weak marks that hardly hold their own on the paper. Yet the same pastels, used freely and with imagination, are capable of creating strong, exciting images that are as accessible to beginners as they are to experienced artists.

▷ **Blending with water** *Pastel can be blended with water applied with a soft brush. The effect is similar to that of watercolour or gouache and is often used to achieve a strong, bright underpainting.*

▷ **Texture with water** *For a more textural effect, apply the water in short, irregular strokes. This technique transforms patches of pastel into dashes of solid, bright colour which look like strokes of gouache.*

### The underpainting

Using paint instead of pastel for the underpainting can effectively get you over the problem of starting, because it creates an area of bold, solid colours on which to apply the pastels. Acrylic, gouache or poster colour are good because they are opaque and quick-drying.

Another way to safeguard against a weak beginning is to dissolve and spread the initial pastel drawing with water or turpentine. Turpentine makes the support slightly greasy and produces an unusual, almost waxy effect as the dry pastel is applied over the turpentine-covered surface. This effect can be seen in the landscape project on pages 64–9, in which the artist uses the turpentine to enrich and strengthen some of the undercolours.

If you plan to use water, paint or turpentine, the support must be strong enough to take the wetting. This means either mounting your pastel paper on a stiff cardboard backing, or using heavy watercolour paper or card for your painting.

### Darkening with fixative

Fixative, generally used to prevent pastels from smudging, is also useful for darkening tones and giving a boost to colours which look too pale and powdery. There is no need to fix the whole picture; just spray those areas you want darker. If you intend to carry on working the darkened areas, use the fixative lightly. Too much will seal the surface, making it unworkable. Some artists actually dip the pastel stick into the fixative and then apply the moist, darkened colour directly to the painting.

**Gouache underpainting**

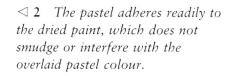

◁ **1** *Gouache or any other water-based paint can be used as a base for pastels. Here the artist starts by applying an area of solid gouache colour.*

◁ **2** *The pastel adheres readily to the dried paint, which does not smudge or interfere with the overlaid pastel colour.*

## PROJECTS

# DAISIES AND DAHLIAS

### Pastel with paint

Many artists put in the background and main shapes with paint – a bright, solid foundation which is quick and easy to apply. You can use watercolour, gouache, acrylic or other quick-drying paint. Watercolour is transparent and generally produces a pale, wash-like under-painting. Gouache and acrylic are both opaque and will provide a bolder base. A bold underpainting is ideal if you are nervous about starting – many beginners are over-cautious.

Work quickly on the underpainting, ideally with a small decorator's brush or the biggest oil-painting brush you can find, establishing main subject and background areas with broad, vigorous strokes. Chunky brushes and a strict time-limit of only a few minutes will encourage you to work in large areas of colour. If you use a tiny watercolour brush, you will be tempted to fiddle with neat outlines and too much detail.

### Starting colours

Colourwise, there are two approaches to underpainting. You can do as the artist did in this flower composition and choose colours that relate directly to the actual subject. The underpainted daisies are white and yellow; the dahlias, red; and so on. The subsequent pastels then develop the subject and introduce the light and dark tones.

A second method of underpainting is to use complementary, or opposite, colours. The red flowers would initially be painted green; the daisies black, and so on. Use pastels to apply the local colours over the contrasting base. You should allow tiny flecks of contrasting undercolour to show through the pastel colours. You will be surprised at how these contrasting specks intensify the overall colours.

△ 1   *The support used for this flower painting is heavy, rough watercolour paper. A white support is not generally recommended for pastel work. However, it will work in this case because the artist intends to lay down an overall acrylic underpainting before applying the pastel. Here the artist is starting to block in the subject with diluted acrylic paint.*

△ 2   *Continue blocking in all the main shapes in their approximate local colours. Ideally, each painted area should be slightly lighter or darker than the actual subject. This will help the subsequent pastel painting to show up against a slightly contrasting background.*

△ **3** *The underpainting is now complete and the painting is ready to be developed in pastel. Washy black is used on the background because the artist intends to work over this later with a denser black pastel. The painted background is taken right up to the edge of the flowers and completely eradicates the white of the paper.*

△ **4** *Starting with the yellow flower centres, the artist works on to the dried underpainting with pastel.*

◁ **5** *The dahlias are developed in mid-pink. Because the acrylic undercolour is slightly darker than the pastel pigment, the petals show up as separate shapes. Yet the underpainting is close enough to the pastel colour not to spoil or dominate the subtle pink of the petals.*

△ 6   The picture so far has been partially developed with pastel. Some of the leaves and stems have now been drawn and the position of the smaller flowers dotted in over the background. Paler highlights have been added to the pink petals and the artist has developed the yellow daisies in the same way. Again, the petal colour differs just enough from the yellow of the underlying acrylic to allow the flower heads to show up against their background.

▷ 7   For the white flower petals the artist presses hard on the pastel to ensure a solid, opaque colour. The pastel petals are extended over the edge of the underpainted shape, giving each petal a clear, crisp shape that stands out against the darker tones behind.

▷ 8   Some of the background is chalked in before the smaller flowers are painted. Because pastels are so opaque, it is possible to lay white over a much darker colour, as the artist has done with these daisies. Here the background is being touched up around the flowers. Although the background looks black, it is actually Payne's grey – the artist felt black would look too harsh.

△ 9 *Payne's grey is used around some of the shapes which have become indistinct and smudgy during the working.*

◁ 10 *Care was taken not to overwork this painting because the artist wanted to retain the freshness and spontaneity of the original underpainting. There is no fussy detail in the flowers, and the background is left deliberately sketchy – much livelier than a flat tone or colour. In nature flowers and leaves are never completely regular and are rarely seen from a full frontal view, so the artist was careful to avoid too much symmetry in this picture, either in the subject or in the composition as a whole.*

# PROJECTS

# LANDSCAPE IN FRANCE

### Dissolving the underpainting

Pastels are soluble and once they have been applied you can blend them with water or turpentine. To do this, use a brush or a tissue. The immediate effect is to create a smudgy, wash-like area of colour that can then be developed using dry pastel sticks.

For the newcomer to pastels, blending the first stages in this way has the same advantages as paint. It gives you a bold, overall colour on which to work. The dissolved underpainting may then be covered completely as you develop the picture or, more usually, some areas will be allowed to show through to provide a contrasting texture in the finished painting.

If you use water to blend pastel, the pigment will darken at first but then dry to its original colour. Turpentine, on the other hand, enriches the colours, which then tend to dry permanently darker but rather patchily – an effect which many artists like because this can lift an otherwise dull area in the picture, particularly empty background expanses and other large spaces.

There were two such areas in this colourful landscape subject: the field and the sky. The artist dissolved the initial colour on these areas with turpentine and then immediately worked over the wet areas with dry pastel. This produced a very particular effect because the overlaid pastel absorbed the turpentine on the surface of the support, giving the colours a rich sheen, quite unlike the normal chalky appearance of pastels.

The boldness of the underpainting sets the tone for the rest of the picture, which is then developed with dry pastel sticks. Patterns and textures, such as the field of flowers and furrowed hillside, are indicated with vigorous strokes of strong colour in contrasting tones.

▷ **1** *The artist started by quickly blocking in the local colours of the landscape, using the side of the stick for the larger areas. Colours are light ultramarine for the sky; olive green for the trees; mauve, lizard green, yellow green and yellow ochre for the fields. The pastels are Rowney, which are soft but not excessively so. The support for this landscape is a sheet of cardboard – strong enough to withstand a good soaking of turpentine without buckling.*

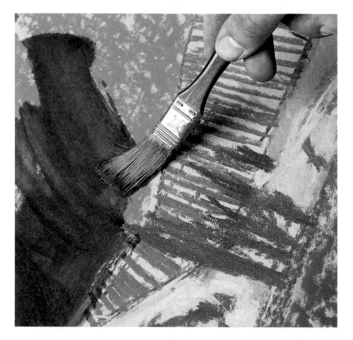

◁, ◁ **2 and 3** *Using a large soft brush, the artist applies turpentine across the area of the sky and lavender field, dissolving the colour, which darkens immediately as the turps sinks into the cardboard. The broad, rugged brushstrokes are deliberate, and the resulting patchy underpainting plays an important role in the next stages.*

▷ **4** *Turpentine has been applied selectively, to the two largest areas. The rest of the picture remains as blocks of broad, dry pastel, ready for further development. The wet areas provide a base for further pastel textures so there is no need to be too precise. The colours will inevitably be uneven at this stage.*

▷ 5　*With a very light ultramarine blue, the artist works into the wet turpentine, using short, dense strokes. The wet surface is slightly slippery to work, and as the dry pastel colour absorbs the turpentine, the picture surface takes on a smooth, satin-like appearance.*

▽ 6　*The effect of the random underpainting shows up in the completed sky, which has a naturalistic mottled appearance and a shinier surface texture than the surrounding pastel colour. The darker sky tones are those where the pastel has picked up the heavier strokes of pigment in the wet underpainting.*

△ 7   As the painting continues, each area and element of the landscape is treated in a very straightforward manner, as a separate, flat pattern or texture. Here, the artist draws the furrows as simple, yellow stripes.

▷ 8   The flat, pattern-like treatment of each area is made possible by the fact that the subject itself contains features which describe the space and distance in the landscape. For instance, the yellow stripes of the distant field create a sense of space, because the lines themselves have a perspective which causes them to recede towards the horizon. Thus the picture emerges as a real scene rather than a mere patchwork of patterns.

△ **9**   *The mauve of the lavender field is still wet as the artist scribbles in rows of pale flowers on to the darker base. As with the sky, the new colour is received patchily and, again, this gives a naturalistic appearance to what is actually a flat texture.*

▷ **10**   *Here the artist is blending the pastel with his finger. The hard outline on the hill is rubbed back to merge with the sky. By making the horizon less distinct, the artist emphasizes the sense of space already established in the painting.*

▷ **11**   *In this close-up photograph, the importance of the direction of the pastel strokes can be seen. Notice how the pale-yellow stubble is created by using long hortizontal strokes across the surface, with a row of short diagonal strokes to indicate the height of the stubble.*

▷ **12** *Seen from a slight distance, these basic pastel marks become a convincing part of the image they represent. For instance, random dots become flower heads, stripes become furrows or rows of foliage, and so on.*

▽ **13** *The completed picture was painted in Hooker's green, mauve, yellow ochre, yellow green, sap green, raw umber, cobalt blue, bright green, lizard green, purple, olive green, burnt umber, cadmium yellow, lemon yellow, raw sienna, green grey and purple grey. Some of the colours, such as yellow ochre, were used in several tones.*

# CHAPTER 5 CHAPTER

# Advanced pastel

*T*O GET the most out of the flexibility of pastels, it is a good idea to explore different ways of applying colour so that you can overlay the pigments, creating and controlling almost any effect you wish to achieve.

Overlaid, or broken, colour means that you are using two or more colours in such a way that they can both be seen, and both contribute to the general overall effect. There are many ways of doing this. For instance, impasto, or thick colour, can be built up, as with other mediums, so that the actual texture of the pastel plays an important part in the finished painting.

Similarly, you can 'glaze' with pastels, creating a transparent layer. Like impasto, this is an oil-painting term. It describes the overlaying of veil-like layers of transparent colours so that the colours mix. In paints you do this by diluting. In pastels you do it by applying a colour very thinly with the length of the stick.

The artist involved in this part of the book had tremendous fun with textures, particularly with a technique known as frottage, which is similar to brass-rubbing. You can be inventive and use unusual and unconventional materials. You are not confined to a traditional, classical approach.

*Loose, lively strokes give this colourful landscape a feeling of freshness and movement. The artist, Graham Painter, is predominantly a landscape painter and uses layers of overlaid pastels to capture the colours and atmosphere of nature.*

# OVERLAID COLOUR

Depending on the support you use, it is possible to build up many layers of pastel colour before the surface becomes so smooth that it cannot hold any more pigment.

Pastels are opaque and the harder you press, the denser the colour you get. A dark colour applied firmly over a paler colour will generally obliterate the lighter, underlying one. But if you lay a light colour over a darker or brighter colour, the underlying one will usually show through and affect the colour of the pale pastel.

The only way to get rid of unwanted dark colour is to erase it or, if the pastel has been fixed and you are dealing with a small area only, carefully to scrape it away with a scalpel blade.

## Broken colour

Some of the most beautiful pastel paintings are those in which the colour has been built up layer upon layer in such a way that all underlying colours are visible in the finished picture.

This effect can be achieved by using broken

▷ **Hard over soft**  *A hard pastel can be applied over a softer one provided that there is not too much colour already on the support. As layers of pastel build up, you will find it increasingly difficult to do this.*

▷ **Soft over hard**  *Generally it is easier to persuade soft pastel colour to adhere to harder pastel colour. This is especially useful in the early stages of a work, when it is usual to use hard pastel for the initial, linear drawing and then to apply subsequent solid colour with soft pastel.*

colour – applying the pastel in short or light strokes so that it does not completely cover the colour or colours underneath. Alternatively, you could adopt a glazing technique, similar to that used in oil painting. With pastels, glazed colour is applied so thinly that it is transparent and you can see the colour underneath.

### Hard and soft

One of the nicest things about pastels is their flexibility. There is no rigidly correct way to use them, and the only real restrictions are those imposed by the limitations of the pastels themselves. Hard and soft pastels are inter-changeable, and you can use them both in the same painting. Many artists prefer hard pastels for making lines and defining details, and softer ones for broader areas of colour.

That said, it is always easier to use soft pastels over hard than the other way round, especially in the later stages of a painting when the surface of the support starts to clog. An area of soft pastel may resist further working with a hard pastel but still be receptive to more layers of soft colour.

A good general guide is to choose harder pastels in the early stages, especially for the initial drawing, when they are at their most useful. Then use them as often as you want or until it becomes difficult. After all, a hard pastel is not essential for fine work. The jagged edge of a broken pastel is just as good for thin lines, and can achieve considerable detail.

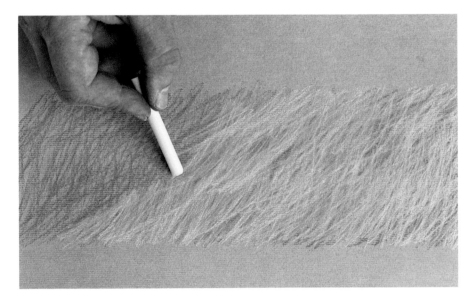

◁ **Feathering**  *Light feathery strokes allow you to mix colours without blending them. Here the artist is lightening dark blue by feathering with strokes of a paler tone.*

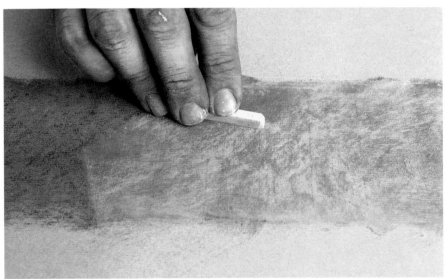

◁ **Glazing**  *Using the side of the pastel, you can overlay layers of thin, transparent colour to get an effect similar to that of glazing with oil paints. In this demonstration, yellow is glazed over red to create orange.*

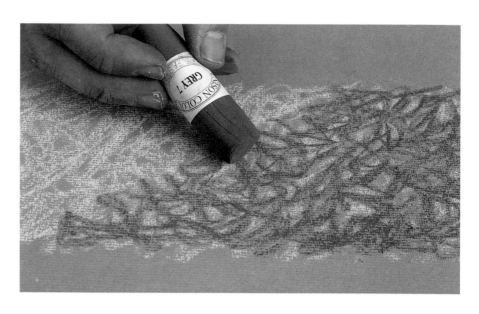

▷ **Broken colour** *The term 'broken colour' is a general one, used to describe any textured stroke that allows the undercolour to show through. Here the artist uses the edge of the pastel stick to lay blue over a much lighter blue.*

▽ **Chunky texture** *Another area of broken colour is created, this time using the width of the pastel stick. Patches of underlying violet show through the pale pink.*

**Impasto**
▽ **1** *Another oil-painting term 'impasto', means thick colour. Soft pastels enable you to build up layers of thick, opaque colour while at the same time allowing flecks of the underlying colours to show through.*

△ **2**  *A third layer of thick, soft pastel is applied here. The top colour, pale blue, is dominant, but the underlying dark and mid-blue are left visible to create an area of rich, broken tone.*

**Scribble pattern**
△ **1**  *A loose scribble is an effective and speedy way of applying and overlaying colour. Here the artist starts with an area of randomly scribbled blue.*

◁ **2**  *Pale green scribbled over the blue produces a broken greenish-blue which could, if necessary, be developed further, with each newly scribbled layer contributing to the final colour.*

TECHNIQUES

# CONTRAST AND COMPLEMENT

Certain colour combinations can create harmony or clashing contrast, depending on the effect you wish to achieve. A bright colour painted over an equally bright one can vibrate in the eye of the viewer, creating an effect that is almost violently bright. In comparison, a single, unbroken colour, however brilliant, will look almost muted.

The colours in this nasturtium painting are exceptionally vivid and compelling. This has happened not because of the bright pastels used by the artist, but because she has used these colours in such a way that they react together, creating an optical effect that makes the colours dance and vibrate as you look at them.

### The technique
Her technique is to overlay the colours so that the final painting has flecks and dots of an equally vivid underpainting showing through. The red and orange of the flower heads, for instance, are worked over two other colours, violet and green, both of which appear as minute specks in the finished picture. They are scarcely visible, but their presence has the effect of making the nasturtiums in the painting as vivid and luminous as they appear in nature.

▷ *A single nasturtium is seen in its various stages. The underpainting, in unnatural violets and greens, looks strangely unreal, but this is developed until the flower and leaf emerge in their brilliant natural colours. Flecks of the underpainting, peeping through, cause the final colours to vibrate in the viewer's eye and make the red and green look particularly vivid.*

### Complementaries
The most effective colour combinations are those pairs of colours found opposite each other in the colour wheel: the complementaries.

The illustration on page 39 shows the colour wheel with the primary colours – red, yellow and

blue – and how these are mixed to get the secondary colours – green, violet and orange. Each of these colours has a 'complementary', the colour immediately facing it on the wheel. Thus the complementary of red is green; yellow, violet; and blue, orange.

What might at first seem rather like useless theory has, in fact, a very practical purpose. The complementary colour pairs work optically together to produce particularly vibrant effects; thus violet placed next to orange, for instance, lends a greater emphasis to both colours, making each seem more vivid and vibrant than it would if used separately.

If you look at any successful painting, in any medium, you will find more often than not that complementary colours have been used to some extent. It is no accident that the underlying colours of these nasturtiums include green and blue, the direct complementaries of red and orange. This was a deliberate choice on the part of the artist, who wanted the flowers to look as brilliant and jewel-like as her pastel colours would allow.

## PROJECTS

# AFRICAN VIOLETS

### Broken colours

Light and colour are the most important elements in this flower painting. To achieve these, the artist has relied on two classical techniques: the use of complementaries, and the application of pastel in short strokes of broken colour. The result is a brilliant image built up with contrasting flecks of colour which are repeated throughout the painting, unifying the elements within the picture and making them glow.

Classical painting involves building up the picture simultaneously. You do not finish one area in detail before moving on to the next because this would make it difficult to relate colours and tones or achieve a unified image. It is far better to keep your options open by developing the picture as a whole, moving from one area to another and making changes until the picture works overall.

Working with broken colours enables this artist to use pastels in the classical tradition. By building up the picture in strokes, she can move from one element to another, making adjustments until each colour, shape and tone works with the others.

### Background colours

The background is not a single colour, or even two colours. It is an overlaid mixture of many warms and cools, all of which echo colours used elsewhere in the painting.

If you overlay two colours or use them next to each other, they react optically. With complementaries, for instance, the colours together look brighter and more luminous than they would if used separately. The effect is similar even when you use paler tones of the complementaries, as the artist has done in this background. Thus pink and light green, used with pale orange and pale blue, make the background a luminous and living area.

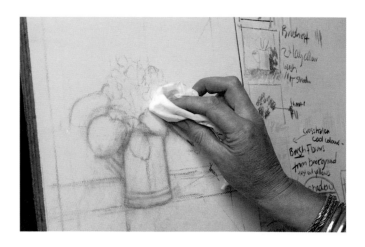

△ 1   *Working on Canson Mi-Teintes paper, the artist starts by making a line drawing in charcoal. The paper is first squared up, and the vase of flowers drawn slightly off-centre to avoid a symmetrical composition. Excess charcoal is wiped off with a tissue.*

▽ 2   *The underpainting is lightly sketched in. Apart from the leaves, all the underpainting is done with the side of the pastel. At this stage, the background is flecked with pink, mauve, yellow and orange, with overlaid strokes of light green; the tablecloth is pink, mauve and light green. Three purples are used for the leaves – a contrasting undercolour for the eventual green – and the mug is pale green.*

△ 3  Starting with the dark rims, the edges of the leaves are defined in viridian green. The artist uses her finger to blend the dark tone, smoothing the colour towards the centre of the leaf. Care is taken not to obliterate the purple underpainting, which will eventually be allowed to show through the green pastel strokes.

▷ 4  The leaves are now quite solidly established in a mixture of greens – mainly viridians and warmer, leafy greens – and the artist moves on to the mug, which is developed in bright yellow.

▽ 5  Before painting the flower heads in a reddish violet, the artist used a stiff brush to remove some of the background colour behind the flowers. This was done to prevent the background colour from mixing with the bright flower colour, and also to clear the support of unnecessary pigment particles. The shadow is blocked in with blue.

△ **6** *A bright blue is used to develop the flowers. The pastel strokes follow the form of the flower heads, and are concentrated mainly around the edges of the petals. As with the rest of the painting, flecks of the underpainting are allowed to show through.*

▷ **8** *Using pinks, yellows, greens and mauves, the artist works into the broken colour of the background. The strokes radiate outwards from the mug of violets. This technique enlivens the background and draws the eye towards the centre of the picture, emphasizing the flowers as the focal point. The background is now paler on the side nearest to the light source.*

◁ 7 *The central elements in the painting – the mug and the violets – have been considerably developed and are now virtually complete. However, as the artist develops the background and the rest of the painting, she will constantly go back to the flowers, adjusting the tones and colours to fit in with their changing surroundings.*

▽ 9 *To lend harmony to the composition and to bring the separate elements together, the same colours are consistently repeated throughout the whole painting. Here, the pale green, already used in the background and foliage, is being added to the mug.*

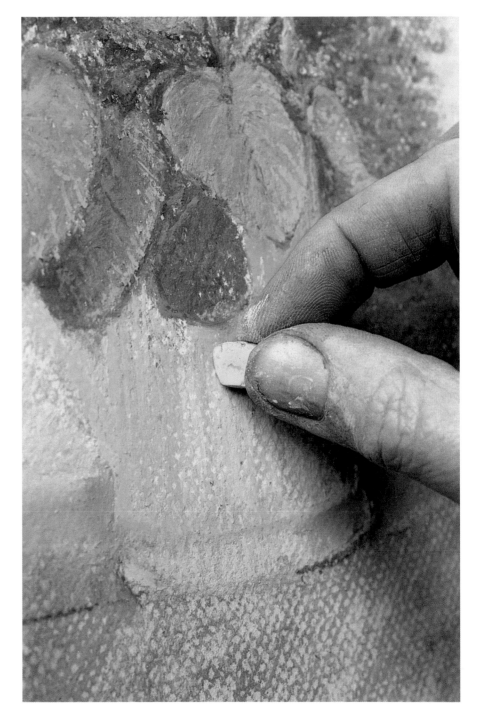

▷ **10** *The effects of the repeated colours can be seen clearly in this close-up. No colour is isolated; rather, all are worked into the overall scheme of broken warms and cools. Flowers, leaves, background, mug and shadow all share the same basic colours, although used in different proportions.*

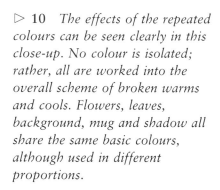

◁ **11** *Even at this late stage it is possible to reduce or change the shape of a painting by brushing away excess pigment. In this case, the artist feels there is too much background and uses a ruler to define the exact picture area by brushing away excess pigment with a stiff brush.*

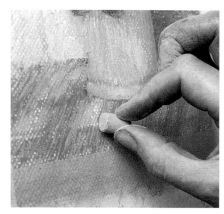

△ **12** *Final touches are added and some of the colours strengthened, bringing them into line with the rest of the painting. Finally the tablecloth is completed in pale purple, pink, blue and green.*

△ **13** *The colours used included pale and warm pinks, pale oranges, pale ceruleans, pale viridians (background); greyish purple, violet, viridian, cool greys (shadow); purple pinks, violets, creamy yellows, viridian (cloth); ultramarine blue, light green, bright yellow, blue and green as shadow (mug); alizarin crimson, leaf, Hooker's and cobalt greens, warm greens, purples (leaves); bright pinky orange, cadmium orange, various violets, viridian green, blue (flowers).*

# TECHNIQUES

# TEXTURE AND PATTERN

Almost any subject you care to choose includes texture or patterns. Sometimes this is a nuisance. A surface texture can make it more difficult to see the overall colour or tone of an object, and it may be better to ignore it. Human hair, the gravel on a garden path, the weave of a certain fabric – all of these are textures that we might decide to leave out in favour of painting the subject in more general terms.

But there are other textures that you may decide to include. They might be too dominant to ignore, or they may enhance the subject; perhaps you just like the texture for its own sake and want to make a feature of it.

You can, of course, use pastel sticks in the classical way, flecking and overlaying the colours to get the effect you want. But pastels are highly adaptable, and there are lots of other ways in which you can achieve different and unusual patterns and textures.

### Frottage

In the painting on page 89, the artist gets a convincing wood grain on the tabletop by laying

△ **Corrugated cardboard** *The artist was able to create this ridged texture by rubbing the pastel over a sheet of corrugated packing card.*

the paper on a wooden floor and scribbling over this with the side of the pastel. The technique is known as 'frottage', and you will probably know of it from church brass-rubbings. It can be used on wickerwork, tree barks, metal mesh and any other raised-surface pattern.

The secret of frottage is not to use it too literally. Be creative. Your tree-bark texture could be used for a background wall area in a still-life painting; a wickerwork pattern might look good as a fabric texture. There are endless possibilities, and you should not be frightened to experiment and try out your own ideas.

## Sgraffito

A scratched pattern is called 'sgraffito', and with this basic technique you can make any amount of textures, fine and coarse. One of its main advantages is that sgraffito can also be used as a salvage operation. An area that has become overloaded, too dense or too dark for the picture, can often be lifted with a scratched pattern rather than risk damaging the paper surface by scraping off layers of colour with a scalpel. A fine point can give you a subtle overall sgraffito texture that can be integrated into the composition and does not overwhelm the rest of the picture: a scalpel or razor blade can produce a coarser effect.

Fixing the pastel can make a difference to the result. If you spray the underlying colours, this will give you a hard surface on to which to scratch, and the bottom colours tend to show up more. Fixing the top surface will result in a clearer, more pronounced scratched pattern.

◁ **Wood grain**  *Bare boards on the studio floor were used for this grained effect, but tree bark, stone and other natural surfaces will produce similarly interesting results.*

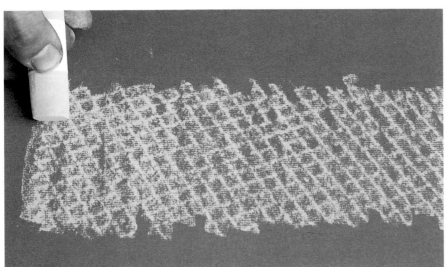

◁ **Metal mesh**  *The protective mesh covering an electric fan produced this grid-like pattern. Netting, basket weave and coarsely woven fabrics are other sources of pattern and texture.*

## PROJECTS

# FISH ON OVAL PLATE

### Cross-hatched colour

In some ways pastel pencils offer the best of two worlds because they are both a drawing and a painting medium. Although harder than pastels, they have some of the soft, malleable quality of pastels in that you can blend colours to create gentle yet vivid effects. But because they are also pencils, they can be sharpened to a point, which means that you can draw fine lines and develop detail in a way that is difficult with pastel sticks.

The composition here is effective in its absolute simplicity. The subject is placed centrally on the paper, and to offset this symmetry the artist uses the yellow tabletop to divide the picture into unequal background areas.

The curved form of the fish is described in tiny patches of cross-hatched colour rendered in well-sharpened pastel pencils. Both the fish and the oval plate are rounded and shiny; the artist was anxious to retain the graphic simplicity of the subject and to avoid too much blending and fuzziness to get the rounded forms.

Pastel pencils and a cross-hatching technique provided the ideal solution. The curved form of the fish is built up in small patches of colour – tiny, separate planes of criss-cross lines that enable the artist to introduce subtle layers of colour into the subject and, at the same time, keep the drawing crisp and accurate.

### Contrasting textures

Softer pastels adhere easily to the pastel pencils, and the two are combined in this picture. In the later stages the highlights and plate were added in broad strokes with a stick of white pastel. These solid, opaque areas contrast with the finer lines elsewhere in the painting, to give a feeling of solidity to the whole image.

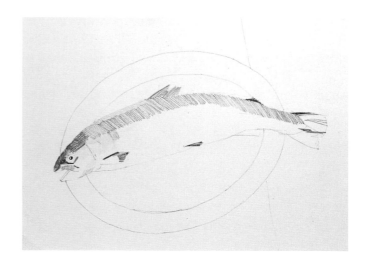

△ 1 *Working on a beige Fabriano pastel paper, the artist starts with a line drawing of the subject. This is done in blue pastel pencil, and the subject is placed centrally on the paper. To establish the fish as a solid object, the artist uses black pencil to hatch a shadow down one side of it.*

▽ 2 *The artist continues blocking in the fish, establishing the rounded form in small, flat planes of light and shade. Each plane is clearly visible. Because there is no attempt to blend the planes, the result is rather like a fish that has been made from folded paper.*

▽ **4**   The rim on the oval dish is hatched with blue. Darker shadow areas are achieved by cross-hatching to create a denser colour.

△ **3**   Colour is introduced into the cross-hatched planes. The artist looks carefully at the actual subject, picking out areas of reflected and local colour.

▽ **5**   The painting so far has been blocked in with pastel pencil alone. The fine cross-hatching technique has given the artist control over the tones, and in areas where the light falls the lines are sparse and thin enough to give the impression of reflected light. In shaded areas, the cross-hatching is dense and dark.

▷ **6** *The side of a white pastel stick is used to establish the broad highlights on the fish. The softer pastel takes easily to the pastel pencils, and the white pigment adheres well to the surface of the support.*

▽ **7** *Similarly, the artist uses the broad side of the white stick to block in the regular line of highlight along the rim of the plate. Again, the soft pigment adheres to the pastel pencil.*

▽ **8** *The white of the plate is blocked in with the soft pastel. This solid tone helps counteract the thin effect of the pastel pencils, and makes the painting look solid and substantial.*

△ 9  *The tabletop takes up a large area of the painting. To make this more interesting, the artist uses a frottage technique to get the effect of wood grain. This is done by placing the paper on the floor and rubbing with the side of a stick of yellow pastel.*

▷ 10  *The completed picture is done in pastel pencils – black, olive green, ultramarine, cobalt blue, dark red, green-grey, Naples yellow, bright yellow, light grey – and white and yellow pastel sticks.*

# TECHNIQUES

# MASKING

The principles of masking are similar to those of stencilling: you cover the area you want to protect from the pastel.

Masking is not an obvious pastel technique, but it is nevertheless useful on occasions, particularly when you want a crisply defined shape or a geometrically straight edge. Masking will give you a hard, defined edge that is otherwise difficult to achieve with pastels.

Pastels are a naturally soft medium, associated more with colour and the quality of light than with hard edges and flat shapes. Many artists who prefer not to use masking in their paintings use it as a matter of course when they tape the edges of the support (see page 30). This is because they like a clearly defined picture area and a good, sharp edge to the painting.

**Sharp edges**

You can get an absolutely straight edge to a shape by masking with the edge of a piece of paper and taking the pastel strokes over it; a torn edge will produce a ragged, irregular shape. Remove the paper mask very carefully by lifting; otherwise the pastel will smudge and these smudges are

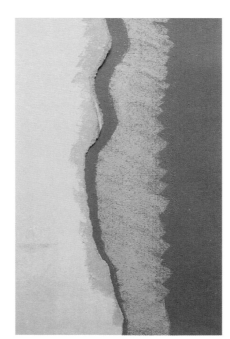

**Masking with torn paper**
△ **1** *The jagged edge of a torn sheet of paper makes a surprisingly effective mask for soft pastels. Hold the paper firmly in place and apply dense strokes of pastel over the torn edge.*

▷ **2** *The mask must be removed carefully without smudging the sharp, clean shape left by the torn paper.*

**Straight edges**
△ **1** *You can create a geometrically straight line by painting over the straight edge of a sheet of stiff paper.*

▷ **2** *Again, the paper mask must be removed very carefully so as not to spoil the precise line of colour.*

particularly conspicuous on otherwise geometric shapes. It is a good idea to fix the painting before placing the paper on it. If you want a broad, straight line, position two sheets of paper to the width you require and fill in the space between the two.

A ruler will give you a similarly straight edge but is less precise, so it is generally best for larger-scale paintings.

### Stencil mask

A more ambitious masking technique is to make a stencil. This involves cutting out the shape or shapes you want from a sheet of paper, placing the paper on the painting and then applying pastel over the cut-out shape. The secret here is to use the pastel lightly, building up the colour or colours in thin layers rather than attempting to lay a thick layer in one go.

Paper masks are fragile and will rip if you use the pastel too energetically. It is generally best to take light strokes from the paper on to the painting. If you do it the other way round, the paper will tear. Dense colour is difficult to obtain, and the technique is most effective when used to create light, feathery effects. Use more than one colour if you want an area of broken colour or a glazed effect.

Masking is always easier if you use fixative, so spray both on the painting before you lay the mask, and on the stencilled shape after you have removed the mask.

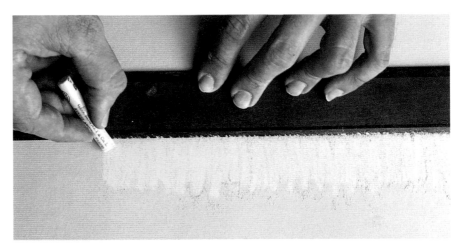

### Using a ruler

△ **1** *A ruler is sometimes used to create a straight, slightly jagged edge. Hold the ruler in place and take the pastel strokes up to the edge of the ruler.*

◁ **2** *The result is coarser than that made with a paper mask but is nevertheless useful for creating rapid edges when working on a reasonably large scale.*

## PROJECTS

# ALICE

Many artists avoid drawing and painting the human figure, presuming it to be complicated and therefore far beyond their capabilities. 'I can't do people!' is the usual response to a human subject, and this is a pity because when painting figures and portraits, your approach and techniques should be exactly the same as for any other subject. There is nothing to be afraid of.

### Figure drawing

Keep the initial drawing as simple as possible. Your subject may have arms, legs and a face, but if you treat these human characteristics as basic shapes and forms, they are actually no more difficult than a still-life subject. The secret is to simplify – just as the artist does in this portrait painting of his daughter, Alice.

Every solid form can be expressed in simple terms of light and shade. For the purpose of your painting, try to imagine the subject as being made of folded paper, rather like an origami figure. In this case, the limbs, face and body cease to be composed of rounded forms; instead, the figure is reduced to easily discernible planes of light and shade.

This is exactly how the artist has tackled this painting of his daughter. The arms, torso and head of the little girl are depicted as flat planes in three main tones – dark, medium and light, and each plane is left as a flat area of hatched colour. No attempt is made to blend these planes together to make them look more 'round' or 'real'.

### The background

The setting, too, is simplified. Alice is standing on the beach with the sea behind her – a background suggested with a minimal block of bright blue to represent the sunlit water, and a sharply defined horizon line which creates an illusion of space and distance.

△ **1** *Working on a pale, neutral paper, the artist starts by lightly sketching the subject in red pastel. The drawing is kept deliberately simple – a light outline sketch that will not interfere with subsequent colours.*

▽ **2** *Cool blue-grey and dark brown are used for the shadow areas, which are simplified into broad planes of dark tone. Notice how the shaded side of the upper arm is indicated as a flat shape of blue-grey; the artist has made no attempt to make the arm look soft and rounded.*

▽ 3   So far the artist has blocked in most of the shaded areas, thus establishing the darkest tones in the picture.

△ 4   Some highlights and other pale tones are now added to the established dark areas. Here, the reflected sunlight in the girl's hair is painted in pale cream. To avoid smudging the picture as he works, the artist places a sheet of clean paper over complete areas.

▽ 5   At this stage, the medium flesh tones – warm oranges and reds – have been added in simplified areas. Again, the pastel has been applied and the figure is now almost complete.

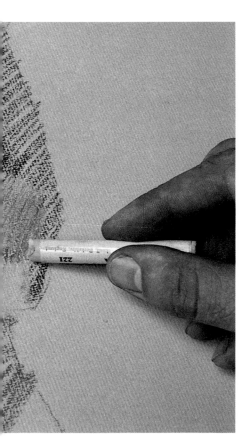

▷ **6** *The lightest tones of the subject, the facial highlights, are established in very pale pink.*

▽, ▷ **7 and 8** *Close-up photographs of the girl's face and body reveal the subtle use of warm and cool colours in this figure painting. Flesh tones have been simplified into light, medium and dark colours. The darkest tones – the shadows – are predominately cool; mid-tones and highlights are applied in warm orange, pink, brown and red.*

◁ **10**  Bold blue pastel strokes are taken over the edge of the paper mask which is then carefully peeled back to reveal the straight edge of the horizon.

◁ **9**  The outdoor setting shows the subject against a bright blue sea with a clearly defined horizon. Here the artist uses the straight edge of a sheet of paper as a mask in order to achieve the crisp line of the horizon.

▷ **11**  In the finished picture, the pale, warm tone of the support is left to represent the sky colour. The same tone can also be seen between the hatched flesh tones of the figure, thus creating a harmonious link between the subject and background.

# INDEX